DISPARITIES IN URBAN HEALTH

T0094122

DISPARITIES IN URBAN HEALTH

The Wounds of Policies
and Legal Doctrines

EDWARD V. WALLACE

JOHNS HOPKINS UNIVERSITY PRESS | *Baltimore*

© 2024 Johns Hopkins University Press
All rights reserved. Published 2024
Printed in the United States of America on acid-free paper
9 8 7 6 5 4 3 2 1

Johns Hopkins University Press
2715 North Charles Street
Baltimore, Maryland 21218
www.press.jhu.edu

Library of Congress Cataloging-in-Publication Data

Names: Wallace, Edward V., author.
Title: Disparities in urban health : the wounds of policies and legal doctrines /
    Edward V. Wallace.
Description: Baltimore, Maryland : Johns Hopkins University Press, 2024.
Identifiers: LCCN 2022014727 | ISBN 9781421445694 (paperback) |
    ISBN 9781421445700 (ebook)
Subjects: MESH: Health Status Disparities | Urban Health | Minority Health |
    Health Policy | Social Determinants of Health | United States
Classification: LCC RA563.M56 | NLM WA 300 AA1 |
    DDC 362.1089—dc23/eng/20221128
LC record available at https://lccn.loc.gov/2022014727

A catalog record for this book is available from the British Library.

Special discounts are available for bulk purchases of this book. For more informa-
tion, please contact Special Sales at specialsales@jh.edu.

CONTENTS

James B. Stewart
Professor Emeritus
Penn State University

Edward Wallace's systematic examination of the causes and consequences of urban health disparities is especially timely. There is a critical need for policy guidance as the United States and the rest of the world continues to grapple with the consequences of the COVID-19 pandemic. Although Wallace's research was conducted prior to the pandemic's onset, his analysis and recommendations provide useful direction for efforts to recover from the pandemic's devastating social impacts. It is well documented that the ruination propagated by the pandemic has been disproportionately borne by African Americans and other marginalized groups.

Data from the Centers for Disease Control and Prevention released in April 2021 indicate that since the onset of the pandemic, African Americans were about 10% more likely to have contracted COVID-19 than non-Hispanic white Americans. However, African Americans were 2.8 times as likely to have been hospitalized after contracting COVID-19 and 1.9 times as likely to die after contracting the disease. For Hispanics, the infection rate was twice as great, the hospitalization rate three times as great, and the mortality rate 2.3 times larger than for non-Hispanic white Americans.[1]

Disparities in health care coverage contribute significantly to disparities in hospitalization and death rates. As an example, Black workers are 60% more likely to be uninsured than white workers, are less likely to have paid sick days, and have less ability to work from home than white workers.[2] Racial segregation and housing discrimination also play important roles in generating differences in the likelihood of contracting COVID-19. Several studies have documented that members of racial/ethnic "minority" groups who contracted COVID-19 were more likely to live in areas with higher population density and more housing units or inadequate housing (such as lack of indoor plumbing).[3]

The greater likelihood of having underlying health conditions, many of which result from historically conditioned disparities in the social determinants of health, also fuel disparities in negative COVID-19 outcomes. Higher obesity rates of Blacks and Hispanics, as well as higher blood pressure and a greater prevalence of diabetes, have all contributed to disproportionate hospitalization and mortality rates.[4]

While it is absolutely critical to carefully scrutinize the mounds of empirical data documenting significant health disparities, it is equally important to remember that there are human faces attached to the numbers. The methodology and mode of presentation used by Wallace brings the human misery generated by health disparities to the forefront. He employs an innovative synthesis of information from reputable scientific sources, narrative descriptions of difficulties experienced by individual families, and his own personal experiences to amplify important findings. The nine hypothetical families that he highlights are composite representations of actual families that he interviewed in the course of his research. The use of this type of composite character is sometimes used in literary works—for example, in the novels authored by W. E. B. Du Bois.[5] Each of the composite families is used to foreground particular dimensions of the overall nexus of factors contributing to systemic health disparities.

These compositely constructed families are used to examine a variety of issues in the book's seven chapters. The second chapter scrutinizes environmental hazards that disproportionately impact inner-city urban residents. Well-known environmental dangers such as air pollution and proximity to brownfields are discussed, as well as less closely examined problems such as exposure to rodents and cockroaches. Although not included in Wallace's analysis, research has also documented that urban heat islands exacerbate health problems. Heat islands are locales that experience above-average daytime temperatures, reduced nighttime cooling, and higher air-pollution levels. These factors in-duce heat-related deaths and illnesses, including respiratory difficulties, heat cramps, heat exhaustion, and non-fatal heat strokes.[6]

The third chapter zeroes in on oral health challenges. Although oral health tends to receive less attention than other health issues, it is impor-tant to recognize that poor oral health potentially contributes to sev-eral diseases and conditions, including endocarditis, cardiovascular disease, pregnancy and birth complications, and pneumonia.[7] Wallace appropriately targets the lack of access to dentists in urban areas and the unwillingness of many to treat Medicaid recipients as important contributors to oral health disparities.

The role of poverty, per se, in cementing health disparities is the sub-ject of the fourth chapter. The historically large gap between the poverty rates of Blacks and Hispanics compared to those of whites persists. In 2018, the poverty rates for Black and Hispanic families were, respec-tively, 18.8% and 16.1%, compared to 5.7% for non-Hispanic white families. Although the poverty rates for Black and Hispanic families reached all-time lows in 2019 (16.9% and 14.4%, respectively), the gap between these rates and those of non-Hispanic white families (4.9%) declined only slightly.[8]

Without a substantial injection of federal assistance, the pandemic would have dramatically increased the poverty rates for all groups. The Urban Institute estimates that without any public intervention, the 2020 poverty rates for Black, Hispanic, and non-Hispanic white individuals (not families) would have been 20.5%, 18.2%, and 9.0%, respectively. As a result of the federal stimulus payments, expanded unemployment assistance, and other economic money payments, the 2020 poverty rate for individuals in each group is projected to be, respectively, 15.2%, 13.7%, and 9.2%.[9]

These figures highlight one of the central points emphasized by Wal-lace in chapter 5—that is, that there are formidable legal and other structural barriers that inhibit a systematic approach to poverty reduc-tion. Even though large amounts of temporary assistance were provided to individuals and families in response to the pandemic, many people were still left in dire straits. There is no systematic plan in place to

prevent the most vulnerable from experiencing catastrophic disloca-
tions after the temporary assistance ends.

The implications of the absence of a societal commitment to provide
adequate health care to all citizens is explored in chapter 6. Wallace introduces the concept of the "Damaging Constitution" to emphasize the
fact that the country's founding document "does not require local and
state governments to provide any good or services to the public whatsoever, unless they want to." The absence of mandated national norms
has catalyzed gross geographical disparities in the availability and quality of medical services. As an example, urban hospitals serving disproportionate percentages of Black and Latino patients have been closed
in several cities. Many of the patients using these facilities have been
forced to use emergency rooms as an alternative to primary health care
providers.[10] Wallace also uses this chapter to underscore the limited access to mental health services available to inner-city residents. Here, he
reminds readers about the prevalence of "historical trauma" experienced
by Black Americans, which requires a distinctive approach to remedia-
tion that addresses "how traumatic events impact a group of people
rather than the individual."

Chapter 6 examines various government programs that provide funding for inner-city residents with lower incomes, including Temporary
Assistance for Needy Families (TANF), Medicaid, and the Earned Income Tax Credit. TANF was introduced in 1996 to replace the former
Aid to Families with Dependent Children (AFDC) program. This is the
primary cash assistance program for families with the lowest incomes.
According to Safawi and Floyd, TANF "is at its weakest point in the
program's history in most states."[11] They find that "In 33 states, benefit
levels have declined by at least 20 percent in inflation-adjusted value
since TANF's enactment."[12] Moreover, the authors insist, "in *every* state,
benefits are at or below 60 percent of the poverty line and fail to cover
rent for a modest two-bedroom apartment."[13] These authors also find
that "TANF does a poor job of providing assistance to Latino and especially Black children," continuing a pattern established under the
AFDC program whereby "many states with high Black populations
kept AFDC benefits very low."[14]

Despite the efforts of former President Donald J. Trump, the number of states that increased participation in the Medicaid program expansion under an initiative orchestrated during the Obama administration has grown. As of this writing, there are only 12 states that have not expanded their Medicaid program to cover more residents living in poverty (Alabama, Florida, Georgia, Kansas, Mississippi, North Carolina, South Carolina, South Dakota, Tennessee, Texas, Wisconsin, and Wyoming). In February 2021, a bill was introduced in the House of Representatives that would provide new incentives for states to expand Medicaid coverage to an additional 4 million individuals.[15] Another bill was also introduced in the House in February 2021 that would expand the Child Tax Credit and the Earned Income Tax Credit. If enacted, this proposal is projected to lift over 4 million children out of poverty and reduce the number of children living in poverty by 40%.[16] The most far-reaching proposed legislation introduced in early 2021 is the Medicare for All Act of 2021. If enacted, this legislation would guarantee health care to everyone in America as a human right and provide comprehensive benefits to all with no copays, private insurance premiums, deductibles, or other cost-sharing.[17]

In the book's final chapter, Wallace informs readers that he has described two very different worlds. One world is inhabited by his composite families, who constantly face health challenges created over time by "policies and legal doctrines [that] have historically harmed these families for decades." The other world is aspirational and "unified in creating health policies and health equity for all people despite race, ethnicity, and socioeconomic status uncertainties regarding how those challenges will be overcome." Wallace suggests that this second world is slowly coming into being, but will require a significant increase of social empathy to blossom fully. He also recognizes that sustained advocacy by supporters of alternative health care policies will be absolutely critical for his second world to become a reality.

Readers of *Disparities in Urban Health* will certainly have the requisite information to play an important role in fighting for policies that ameliorate the gross health care and health outcome inequities that are dysfunctional features of Wallace's first world. In addition, by advocating actively for the enactment of the 2021 legislative proposals discussed previously, they will be contributing directly to the creation of Wallace's second world.

Notes

1. Centers for Disease Control and Prevention, "Risk for COVID-19 Infection, Hospitalization, and Death by Race/Ethnicity," updated March 25, 2022, https://www.cdc.gov/coronavirus/2019-ncov/covid-data/investigations-discovery /hospitalization-death-by-race-ethnicity.html#print.
2. Valerie Wilson, "Inequities Exposed: How COVID-19 Widened Racial Inequities in Education, Health, and the Workforce," Testimony before the US House of Representatives Committee on Education and Labor, Economic Policy Institute, last updated June 22, 2020, https://www.epi.org/publication/covid-19 -inequities-wilson-testimony/.
3. See Alexis K. Okoh, Christoph Sossou, Neha S. Dangayach, Sherin Meleda-thu, Oluwakemi Phillips, Corinne Raczek, et al., "Coronavirus Disease 19 in Minority Populations of Newark, New Jersey," *International Journal for Equity in Health* 19, no. 93 (2020), https://doi.org/10.1186/s12939-020-01208-1; and Desi Rodriguez-Lonebear, Nicolás E. Barceló, Randall Akee, and Stephanie Russo Carroll, "American Indian Reservations and COVID-19: Correlates of Early Infection Rates in the Pandemic," *Journal of Public Health Management and Practice* 26, no. 4 (2020): 371–77, https://doi.org/10.1097/phh .0000000000001206.
4. See Maher El Chaar, Keith King, and Alvaro Galvez Lima, "Are Black and Hispanic Persons Disproportionately Affected by COVID-19 because of Higher Obesity Rates?," *Surgery for Obesity and Related Diseases* 16, no. 8 (2020): 1096–99, https://doi.org/10.1016/j.soard.2020.04.038; J. Jeremy, A.W. Gold, Karen K. Wong, Christine M. Szablewski, Priti R. Patel, John Rossow, Juliana da Silva, et al., "Characteristics and Clinical Outcomes of Adult Patients Hospitalized with COVID-19—Georgia, March 2020," *Morbidity and Mortality Weekly Report* 69, no. 18 (2020): 545–50, http://dx.doi.org/10.15585/mmwr.mm6918e1; and Vijay Gayam, Muchi Ditah Chobufo, Mohamed A. Merghani, Shristi Lamichhane, Pavani Reddy Garlapati, and Mark K. Adler, "Clinical Characteristics and Predictors of Mortality in African-Americans with COVID-19 from an Inner-City Community Teaching Hospital in New York," *Journal of Medical Virology* 93, no. 2 (2021): 812–19, https://doi.org/10.1002/jmv.26306.
5. See James B. Stewart, "Reaching for Higher Ground: Toward an Understanding of Black/Africana Studies," *The Afrocentric Scholar* 1, no. 1 (1992), 1–63; and "Psychic Duality of Afro-Americans in the Novels of W.E.B. Du Bois" in *Flight: In Search of Vision* (Trenton, NJ: Africa World Press, 2004), 93–106. Originally published in *Phylon* 44, no. 2 (1983), 93–106.

6. United States Environmental Protection Agency, "Heat Island Impacts," last accessed April 30, 2021, https://www.epa.gov/heatislands/heat-island-impacts #health.

7. Mayo Clinic Staff, "Oral Health: A Window to Your Overall Health," last accessed April 30, 2021, https://www.mayoclinic.org/healthy-lifestyle/adult -health/in-depth/dental/art-20047475.

8. US Census Bureau, "Table 2. Poverty Status of People by Family Relationship, Race, and Hispanic Origin: 1959 to 2019," last accessed April 30, 2021, https://www.census.gov/data/tables/time-series/demo/income-poverty/historical -poverty-people.html.

9. Linda Giannarelli, Laura Wheaton, and Gregory Acs, "2020 Poverty Projections," last updated July 2020, https://www.urban.org/sites/default/files/publication /102521/2020-poverty-projections.pdf.

10. Joseph P. Williams, "Code Red: The Grim State of Urban Hospitals," *U.S. News & World Report*, July 10, 2019, https://www.usnews.com/news/healthiest -communities/articles/2019-07-10/poor-minorities-bear-the-brunt-as-urban -hospitals-close.

11. Ali Safawi and Cindy Reyes, "States Must Continue Recent Momentum to Further Improve TANF Benefit Levels," *Center on Budget and Policy Priorities*, updated December 2, 2021, https://www.cbpp.org/research/family-income -support/states-must-continue-recent-momentum-to-further-improve-tanf-benefit.

12. Safawi and Reyes, "States Must Continue Recent Momentum."

13. Safawi and Reyes, "States Must Continue Recent Momentum."

14. Safawi and Reyes, "States Must Continue Recent Momentum."

15. Megan Leonhardt, "Democrats Push for State Medicaid Expansions That Could Benefit Roughly 4 Million Americans," *CNBC News,* February 10, 2021, https://www.cnbc.com/2021/02/10/relief-bill-incentivizes-state-medicaid -expansions-that-could-aid-4-million-americans.html.

16. Chuck Marr, Kris Cox, Stephanie Hingtgen, Katie Windham, and Arloc Sherman, "House COVID Relief Bill Includes Critical Expansions of Child Tax Credit and EITC," *Center on Budget and Policy Priorities*, March 2, 2021, https://www.cbpp.org/research/federal-tax/house-covid-relief-bill-includes -critical-expansions-of-child-tax-credit-and.

17. "Jayapal Introduces Medicare for All Act of 2021 Alongside More Than Half of House Democratic Caucus After Millions Lose Health Care During a Pandemic," Pramila Jayapal, last updated March 17, 2021, https://jayapal.house .gov/2021/03/17/medicare-for-all/.

DISPARITIES IN URBAN HEALTH

ONE

Introduction

NOT MANY people are familiar with the landmark publication *Report of the Secretary's Task Force on Black and Minority Health*, released in 1985.[1] This document marked the first time the health and medical profession openly admitted to the public that there are racial and ethnic disparities in health care. What it did not address, however, was where the people it surveyed were living. That is where my research begins.

I first became interested in health disparities in 1990 when I took an epidemiology course in college. I soon learned that not everyone has the same opportunity to be healthy. In fact, my community was making me sicker. I grew up in the "Boogie Down" Bronx in New York City, in the Edenwald housing project. Edenwald Houses are the largest New York City housing development in the Bronx, consisting of 2,039 apartments that house 4,768 people.[2] We lived on top of one another in a 14-story structure. On any given day, we would encounter the smell of human urine and feces, roach infestations in apartments, loud noises, drug deals, and prostitution. Violence was at an all-time high in the 1980s, and poverty was the norm. We all witnessed—and some even experienced—police harassment of and violence against the people in the Edenwald housing project, and it was widespread.

When I was a senior in college, I accepted a paid internship at the New York State Department of Health as a health inspector and law enforcer. In that role I traveled to a variety of low-income neighborhoods and learned how effective laws were in getting people to do the right thing and protect the people living in those neighborhoods. This ultimately began my career in studying health disparities and wanting to use legislation as a mechanism to prevent the disparities in health status between various populations.

Since the early 2000s, research in health disparities has undergone a paradigm shift. During the first 10 years, the majority of the research focused on describing relevant disparities between white people and other racial/ethnic groups. Since 2010, research has focused on identifying the underlying causes of health disparities and the conditions in which disparities occur (that is, individual behaviors, socioeconomic status, access to quality health care, and geographical location). Research from the mid-part of the decade, 2015 and beyond, contributed toward reducing health disparities by developing, implementing, and evaluating interventions.

Today, the impact of legislative policies on people living in urban neighborhoods has largely been neglected when it comes to disparities in health and medical care. Studies that do address the health of people in low-income neighborhoods usually consider policies based on technological health assessments and digital data, rather than lived individual experiences worthy of independent examination. Likewise, community-based studies that focus on low-income neighborhoods tend to concentrate on social relationships such as faith-based organizations and community health advocacy.

This book is intended to close the gap by allowing families who live in low-income neighborhoods to discuss how their health has been affected, in their own terms, and by studying policies that have created certain obstacles for people with low incomes looking to get and stay healthy. I have lived in and visited many urban cities in the United States, such as Birmingham, Alabama; the Bronx in New York City; Cincinnati, Ohio; Ithaca, New York; Amherst, Massachusetts; Dover, Delaware; and many others. I have seen firsthand how people in low-income urban neighborhoods have benefited or been negatively impacted by legislative policies. In conducting research, I have intertwined policies and legal doctrines with the life experiences of those who are impoverished and vulnerable.

For more than 20 years, I have been compiling large-scale national data related to health disparities affecting more than 69,000 African Americans and Hispanics living in low-income urban neighborhoods in cities across the United States. I am involved with research that focuses on reducing obesity and eliminating health disparities among African Americans living in urban neighborhoods. In addition, I have conducted research on African Americans who suffer from trauma and mental health issues due to their social environment.

Methodology

Throughout the book, I illustrate how low-income families who live in urban neighborhoods are harmed by policies and legal doctrines. I reached out to interviewees through local churches and community organizations, friends and colleagues, and through additional contacts that were recommended by those who were initially interviewed. The participants were chosen by means of the snowball sampling technique—also known as "word of mouth"—whereby a person that you have spoken with tells a friend what it is you are researching, and then that person goes and tells a friend, and so on. This sampling technique was selected because it is the most effective way to recruit participants when asking about sensitive information. Having the various communities advocate for me and trust that I will share their experiences honestly and with dignity was crucial to my research. Without the advocacy and trust of the community, it would have been extremely difficult, if not impossible, for me to go into low-income neighborhoods and speak with participants.

Many of the families I conducted interviews with are African American and Hispanic. Originally, I had drafted written surveys and administered them to the participants. As I reviewed the surveys, however, it became evident that they did not capture the entire story and were not as powerful as using people's actual words. As a result, the surveys were restructured and administered through personal interviews. This approach allowed the participants to tell their stories from their own point of view, which enables others to connect with each family's personal story and life experiences.

In the following chapters, I discuss nine families from my research as well as my own family's life experiences. (To protect the confidentiality and privacy of the participants in my research, the following families are representative composites of actual families I have studied: Worley, Coleman, Ruiz, Hughes, Santoya, Whittredge, Stevenson, Rubio, and Blackmon. In all cases, the full name of each participant has been changed in the book to protect their privacy.) I look at how laws and legal doctrines have impacted the Hughes and Worley families' oral health and how the families have both been affected by poverty in different ways. To provide some context, I talk about the changes that have occurred in the families over time, and I address some big questions: Are health disparities here to stay? Has the responsibility of our government to protect and improve the health status of the country's most vulnerable citizens shifted away from helping families? Why don't our policies address the social conditions in our society that create health disparities? Is lack of coordination within our governmental infrastructures to blame? Can we ensure that public health policies work the same for people who experience poverty as they do for people who are middle-class or wealthy? At its core, this book shows that oftentimes when we create laws, "progress" comes with a cost.

The Hughes Family

When I conducted my research on and made observations about the Hughes family, Regina Hughes worked as a cook in the cafeteria of the school that her younger daughter, Latasha, attended, and Dave Hughes worked as a security guard. Dave and Regina both graduated from high school, but because they often work long hours, they never have time to assist their four children with their schoolwork. Dave and Regina believe in their children getting a good education and making something of themselves. They even went so far as to hire a tutor who was a schoolteacher for more than 35 years and a personal friend of Regina.

All of the children have cell phones and a way of getting in touch with the tutor if they need help with their homework, but they rarely call or ask the tutor for extra help. Samantha, who is the oldest of the children, used to like school a lot until she reached an age when she wanted to hang out with her friends instead. Brandon, who is a year younger than Samantha, and his younger brother, Thomas, both want to sit in their shared bedroom and play video games as soon as they get home from school, even before they finish their homework. Latasha, the youngest sibling, enjoys watching television. No two generations are the same. When my grandmother told me to do something, especially when it came to my schoolwork, there was no time for negotiation. The television was turned off immediately and I was in those books, studying. Dave and Regina, on the other hand, almost have to bribe Latasha to do her schoolwork.

In Samantha's and Brandon's health classes, students do not discuss racial and ethnic health disparities among different populations. Mainly, their curriculums cover sex education and drug use. Samantha and Brandon have never heard of any public health policies.

The family usually starts their morning listening to music as they get ready to have a busy day at work or school. For Dave and Regina, this consists of rhythm and blues. For Samantha, Brandon, Latasha, and Thomas, this means rap music such as Cardi B and Lil Baby.

Both Dave and Regina have jobs where they have very little communication with coworkers. For Dave, this means not being able to talk to anyone about his health, how his children are doing in school, or current events, since his job requires him to stand by the front entrance of the store where he works. Regina's day is a little different: she has coworkers in the kitchen with her, but since her responsibilities consist of cooking 367 free or reduced-cost student lunches for the school, her time for conversation is limited. She does not have a chance to talk about any of her health concerns, such as which dentist she can take her children to when they have a toothache.

At dinner, interactions are much the same. Most nights, Dave and Regina do not ask their children about how they are feeling, whether they are stressed, depressed, or experiencing anxiety while in school. They do not ask their children how they are doing in school academically.

I predict that each member of this family will have a difficult time living a healthy life and climbing out of poverty. Doing well in school never came easily to Dave—he always had a C average in his classes. Will he ever get a promotion at his job? Regina is comfortable as a cook. She would like to go to culinary school, but she has too many bills to pay and feels that she is too old to go back to school. Samantha is not interested in school and not concerned about getting better grades in her classes. She has not taken care of her health; she never exercises and never tries to limit her calories. Brandon has been suspended several times for fighting in school. He skips class regularly and can often be found eating a bag of potato chips. Latasha believes the information that she learns in school is a waste of her time. She refuses to participate in class and disturbs others while in school. Brandon and Thomas enjoy learning but do not have family support from their older sibling or their parents. Brandon and Thomas seem to be very advanced academically for their ages, but there is a strong possibility they may be negatively influenced by other family members about school and may not be able to break the cycle of poverty.

Rosa Santoya

Rosa Santoya was born in Amherst, Massachusetts. She has a younger sister whom she is close to and very protective of at times. Rosa comes from a large, Catholic Puerto Rican family. Even though she has only one sibling, she has a lot of aunts, uncles, and cousins.

Rosa's parents instilled unhealthy eating habits in her at an early age. Many of the meals that her mother prepared for the family were high in starch and sugar, and Rosa and her sister were expected to eat everything on their plate. In Rosa's parents' house, there was an expectation that no food should go to waste. Rosa, as a teenager, was 20 to 30 pounds overweight. She avoided being in high school pictures and would never change into her gym uniform for gym class. During her years in high school, Rosa experienced depression and turned to fast food as a way to cope with her emotional stress.

Ramon Ortiz is Rosa's boyfriend. They have been dating for the past 12 years. During this time, Ramon was incarcerated, and his being in prison has put a strain on their relationship—not just emotionally, but financially as well. Ramon is unemployed and feels pressure to provide for Rosa, but the lasting effects of incarceration and poverty have a tight grip on his future and will not let go.

Rosa comes from a family of cigarette smokers. Rosa's mother and father both started smoking menthol cigarettes at the age of 15 and have been smokers for over 30 years. Rosa's mother tried to stop smoking cold turkey when she was 58 years old, but by then she had already developed cancer.

Eloise Stevenson

Eloise Stevenson is a 68-year-old Black woman who was born and raised in the South. I met Eloise at a Baptist church in Birmingham, Alabama, when a friend invited me to attend Sunday service. Eloise comes from a small family; she is the middle child of three and has two sisters. She has one adult son, whom she hardly sees, and two grandchildren that we will call Ishmael and Elijah. Eloise has helped raise her grandchildren, on her own.

Growing up in the South in a single-parent household, dependent on one income, was a struggle for Eloise and her two sisters. Over the years, Eloise has developed quite a few health problems, including high blood pressure, heart disease, overweight, and anxiety. Her anxiety began as a child when she moved from place to place with her mother and her two sisters, which at times made her feel uncomfortable and nervous. When Eloise was a young girl, she slept with a kitchen knife under her mattress for protection. As an adult, she can be seen displaying the same type of behavior. However, sleeping with a kitchen knife is not something she does every day. Eloise only sleeps with her knife when she is extremely anxious or under a great amount stress. She has not always had a good relationship with her mother. When she was 16 years old, she moved out of her mother's house and lived on the streets of Birmingham. Eloise is very bright, but she never finished high school or went back to school to receive her GED.

The Ruiz Family

Ferdinand and Mercedes Ruiz lived in Puerto Rico for most of their marriage, relocated to Florida, then upstate New York, and finally to the Bronx in New York City in the late 2000s. They do not have any children. In the neighborhood where Ferdinand and Mercedes grew up, the roads were all dirt and there was constant crime. Both Ferdinand and Mercedes attended elementary school, but only Ferdinand went further on. He did not finish high school and never received a GED. While living in Florida, Ferdinand and Mercedes were migrant workers. In the summer they would pick oranges in Florida, and during the fall months they would travel to upstate New York and pick apples. While in upstate New York, Ferdinand made some friends who told him about construction jobs in the Bronx. He took odd jobs doing construction while in upstate New York and, through his hard work, eventually became a carpenter, and he and Mercedes moved to the Bronx.

The Ruizes live in River Park Towers in the Bronx. They own a two-bedroom apartment, which consists of a kitchen, bathroom, and living room. They do not own a car, so Ferdinand uses public transportation to get to and from work every day. The Ruizes often send money to their families back home in Puerto Rico, but this is an economic burden on the couple. Ferdinand and Mercedes primarily speak Spanish, but in their neighborhood the majority of people speak English. Neither Ferdinand nor Mercedes are fluent in English.

Lester and Shelia Blackmon

Shelia Blackmon and her husband, Lester, are an African American couple that have lived all their lives in the Bronx. They have no children together, but from a previous marriage Lester has two daughters and a grandson. For the past year, Lester and Shelia have been living with family members until their new apartment is ready for them to move into. Shelia will be living in the housing project right across from one of her childhood friends. Shelia considers herself to be a very observant individual. As a young girl, she remembers the Black kids not being allowed to eat lunch with the white kids at summer camp. She noticed that every day, when it came time for the kids to have lunch, the white camp staff would allow the white kids to eat first while the Black kids were forced to eat second. When white kids ate first, this meant they had more playing time afterward on the campground. When Shelia asked why the white kids went first all the time, the camp staff explained it was camp policy to make sure kids were behaving in an orderly fashion before they could enter the dining hall to eat lunch. This frustrated Shelia because the white kids were not behaving in an orderly fashion— they were just as loud as the Black kids. As an adult, Shelia continues to notice discrimination, e.g., when people experiencing poverty are denied oral health services.

Life for Lester Blackmon has been rough. Lester had a heart attack that was partially caused by his high blood pressure. Lester has a family history of high blood pressure, and his parents, brother, and sister all have high blood pressure as well. The stress in Lester's life was also a big contributing factor to his poor health, in addition to his lifestyle. He rarely paid any attention to the amount of sodium in the foods that he ate. Lester was employed as an assembly worker at one of the top manufacturing corporations in New York City until he was fired from his job for not showing up to work on time. Lester's older brother had helped him get that job, and now he must try and find another place of employment. Since the loss of his job, Lester has been struggling to make ends meet. His lack of a high school education has been an obstacle to getting a good job. Lester has searched for work but has been rejected because he does not have a bachelor's degree from a college or university.

The Whittredge Family

I met Calvin and Sabrina Whittredge when I moved to the Midwest; they were living in Lincoln Courts, a small public housing apartment complex (which no longer exists) in the West End in Cincinnati, Ohio. The Whittredge family had lived in several low-income housing apartments in different neighborhoods all around Cincinnati. Their first apartment was in Avondale, a predominately African American neighborhood with boarded-up apartment buildings, a lot of illegal drug activity, and not many job opportunities for the residents. Calvin and Sabrina then moved to Roselawn, a low-income neighborhood known for its prostitution, substance abuse, human trafficking, and gun violence. They lived in the Roselawn area for approximately two years before they moved to Over-the-Rhine, a neighborhood that was considered to be one of the "most dangerous neighborhoods" in the United States during the 2001 Cincinnati civil riots, according to the Cincinnati police. The Whittredge family was constantly moving because of the growing shortage of affordable housing in Cincinnati and the lack of jobs that pay a livable wage. Calvin and Sabrina have been married for over 30 years and do not have any children. They spend a lot of time with their niece, Phoebe, who they have helped raise since she was a toddler.

When Sabrina was a teenager, she was very active and enjoyed running. All of the kids in the neighborhood called her a "track star" because she was the fastest girl on the block. She could outrun any girl or boy. Like many other teenagers, Sabrina loved eating fast food and buying candy from the local corner store in her neighborhood. Sabrina knew that eating fast food and candy could cause her to gain weight, but she felt the food was satisfying and made her feel better. Every Friday, when her father got paid, he would give Sabrina and her younger sister five dollars each to get something to eat. Sabrina and her sister would walk down the street, planning how they would spend their money to buy as much food and candy as possible.

As an adult, Sabrina has gotten heavier over the years and constantly gets upset about it. Part of Sabrina's rage is aimed at herself for not taking more responsibility in eating healthy meals when she was a teenager. Another part of her anger comes from the role that Sabrina's environment played in her gaining weight, particularly the growing number of corner stores and the lack of supermarkets in her neighborhood.

Sabrina spends most of her time with her husband, Calvin, who has a disability. She assists him with his daily routine, making sure that he showers and eats three meals. Sabrina prepares his meals with food from the grocery store that contains high levels of sodium. She uses extra salt when she cooks Calvin's meal, even though Calvin has high blood pressure. His high blood pressure has caused him to have major health problems that are difficult for him to manage and have landed him in the hospital on numerous occasions. Although Calvin is enrolled in Medicaid, this has not helped him manage his health challenges.

The Worley Family

Frank and Felicia Worley and their three children, Darryl, Jamal, and Chris, were all living in Birmingham, Alabama, in a housing project when I met them in the 1990s. They had a small three-bedroom apartment that faced the back of the housing unit. They owned two queen-sized beds, a sofa, and a small kitchen table with chairs. Frank worked as a short-order cook, and Felicia was unemployed. The Worleys' children ranged in age from 8 to 15 years old. Darryl, Jamal, and Chris were some of the friendliest children in the neighborhood, always laughing, playing tag, throwing a football, shooting hoops, or riding their bikes in the neighborhood. Jamal did not play sports with the other kids, but children in the neighborhood adored being in his presence because he was kind and giving.

The Worleys watched a lot of television. The majority of the TV programs were sports and cartoons. There were programs available on politics, but the Worleys did not watch or talk about these subjects. Frank and Felicia often worried about their ability to provide adequate food for their three sons. Some days the family had no food to eat. The youngest of the children, Chris, spent most of his time at his friend's apartment next door because his friend's family usually fed him dinner when they had food to spare. Jamal, who was 10, took the early bus to school so he could have breakfast. During lunch, Jamal put a piece of fruit in his book bag so he could have something to snack on when he got home late in the evening. Darryl, who is the oldest, walked around the neighborhood sometimes offering to cut grass or wash people's cars so he could have some money to buy himself some food to eat.

The Rubio Family

The Rubios are a kindhearted, friendly, caring, and sociable family. Josephine Rubio is a single mother who lives in public housing in the Bronx with her 10-year-old daughter, Marisol, and her 14-year-old son, Sebastian. Josephine Rubio and Shelia are childhood friends; they both attended the same high school during the 1980s.

Josephine, a graduate of Evander Childs High School, who never had the opportunity to attend college, works as a waitress at a local diner in her neighborhood. Despite regularly working 40 hours per week and sometimes more, Josephine's wages remain very low, about seven dollars an hour. They live in a two-bedroom apartment. Josephine and Marisol each have a bedroom, and Sebastian sleeps on the living room couch.

Josephine was born in Puerto Rico but moved to New York City with her parents when she was 3 years old. She works hard and is very proud of her Puerto Rican heritage, as she does her best to provide a life for Marisol and Sebastian. Josephine has a tight bond with her two children and is constantly preaching to them that "no one is going to take it easy on them or have sympathy just because they are Puerto Rican." She is a constant fighter against unjust rules and policies and refuses to allow the New York City Housing Authority to take advantage of her and her children just because they are experiencing poverty. Josephine receives housing vouchers meaning she only is responsible for paying 30 percent of her rent and the government pays for the rest. There was an incident where all of the hot water was turned off for all the tenants in Josephine's building. Josephine wondered when the hot water would be turned back on in her apartment. The housing authority shared that they were going to apartments where tenants paid full price for rent before they went to apartments where tenants have vouchers. Sebastian and Marisol get As and Bs in school, and they both have dreams of becoming physicians. Despite their love of learning, Sebastian and Marisol understand the harsh realities of living in poverty in an urban neighborhood. Their mother is not proud of their living conditions, but she hopes that they can become resilient and remain proud Puerto Ricans.

The Coleman Family

The Colemans are a family of four that lives in Dover, Delaware. Richard, Cynthia, and their two children, Pam and Alex, have a three-bedroom apartment. The Colemans receive government assistance. Whenever possible, the family sits around the television and watches political news stations. Richard and Cynthia enjoy talking to their children about politics. They talk about immigration laws and share their thoughts about the Affordable Care Act. They discuss gun laws and the right to bear arms. They have intense conversations about earning a livable wage in the United States. The children discuss how awesome it would be if they were able to go to college for free. Richard and Cynthia push their children to study very hard, and next year, Pam may receive a full academic scholarship for college, if she keeps her grades up and passes her finals.

Conclusion

The neighborhoods in which we are born, live, work, play, pray, and age have a profound effect on how healthy we will be for the remainder of our lives. In this book, I will show how diverse families from low-income urban neighborhoods have strikingly similar problems that result from health policies that make it impossible for people experiencing poverty to achieve good health. I will show how poverty has been treated differently under health policy laws compared to other anti-discrimination laws; demonstrate the connection between poor health and urban neighborhoods; and argue that it is almost impossible for the US government to eliminate health disparities.

Notes

1. Margaret M. Heckler and the United States Department of Health and Human Services Task Force on Black and Minority Health, *Report of the Secretary's Task Force on Black and Minority Health* (Washington, DC: US Dept. of Health and Human Services, 1985).
2. "MyNYCHA Developments," NYCHA Resources, New York City Housing Authority, accessed May 9, 2022, https://my.nycha.info/DevPortal/Portal/DevelopmentData.

TWO

Neighborhood Zip Codes

A More Accurate Determinant of Health

THE WAY in which people live in low-income inner-city neighbor-hoods today—with an abundance of crime, unemployment, drug abuse, and violence, and a lack of family and community support—is only part of the reason that health disparities exist among inner-city dwellers. In my belief, nothing has contributed more to health dispari-ties among African Americans living in inner-city neighborhoods than the physical characteristics of environmental hazards.

One of the ways in which Black people have historically sought a better life for themselves and their families has been to migrate from the South to the North; in fact, more than 6 million Black people mi-grated to northern communities from 1910 to the 1970s.[1] This mass migration is why so many Blacks live in cities such as Cleveland, De-troit, New York City, Los Angeles, and Oakland, California.[2] There are two reasons why such a massive migration took place. The first was the amount of violence that took place in the South against Blacks; the de-mographic geography of this nation as we know it today was shaped by the homegrown terrorism often referred to as lynching. The Black people who migrated north were refugees and exiles fleeing from terror.[3]

The second reason for such a massive migration northward was industrialization. At the turn of the century, depressed agricultural conditions in the South prompted many African Americans to move north and seek industrial jobs in metropolitan areas such as New York, Boston, Chicago, and Philadelphia. However, when many Blacks arrived in the North, they were met with empty promises. Blacks who fled to the North would soon find out that Northern discrimination was no different from Southern discrimination. The hardships of unemployment, low-paying jobs, homelessness, not being able to vote, and unsanitary housing are what Blacks had to endure when they arrived in the North.[4] Both racial terrorism and industrialization came at a cost to the health of African Americans. Before we address how to combat environmental hazards by using the law, let's take a look at the many environmental hazards that have historically impacted people living in low-income urban neighborhoods.

Environmental Hazards: The Air We Breathe in Urban Neighborhoods

Outdoor air pollution has become a serious problem for two primary reasons: (1) an enormous increase in the world's population, especially in urban areas, and (2) since the early 1800s, a rapid growth of energy-intensive industries, which has led to record levels of fossil fuel combustion.[5]

Prior to the twentieth century, if there was any concern about air pollution, it would be associated with the city of London. As early as the thirteenth century, small amounts of coal were shipped to London from Newcastle. As manufacturing companies began to grow, wood supplies diminished and coal burning increased despite the massive outcry by London's citizens, who objected to the smell of coal smoke. In 1661, King Charles II was approached by some of his closest confidants, who complained that it was unhealthy to "breathe the filthy vapors because it corrupted the lungs." In spite of these pleas to the king, coal consumption increased even faster, giving the city of London the notorious slogan, "Where there's muck, there's money."[6] The conditions that made London the air pollution capital of the world began to shift to the United States during the nineteenth and early twentieth centuries. Although air pollution declined in the 1950s and 1960s, due to society's main sources of fuel switching from coal to natural gas and oil, people in cities still had to deal with pollutants—mainly diesel fuel exhaust fumes from automobiles. No longer does anyone have to travel to London to experience respiratory illnesses. Virtually every metropolitan city is grappling with how to deal with deteriorating air quality without interfering with industrial productivity and economic growth.

Today, air pollution is a major problem. A good deal of it stems from overcrowding in our urban neighborhoods, which is the foremost environmental problem we face today and probably the most difficult one to tackle. Historically, there were two main developments that led to the "urban explosion." First was the evolution of culture, which occurred over 600,000 years ago, where groups and individuals learned survival skills to look out for each other while living in communities. Second were the industrial, medical, and scientific revolutions that saw improvements in sanitation and the control of infectious diseases, resulting in the decline of death rates, especially those related to infant mortality. During the 1800s, a mere 6% of all Americans lived in urban areas; the number of city dwellers increased to 15% by 1850 and 40% by 1900. Today, it is estimated that about 54% of Americans live in urban areas, and this number is expected to increase to 66% by the year 2050.[7]

The rapid increase of overcrowding in urban neighborhoods has led to some serious health concerns, such as bronchitis and asthma due to rodent and cockroach infestations. I witnessed this firsthand when I spoke with Felicia Worley about her respiratory illness. Felicia, like many other Black people who live in urban areas and experience poverty, suffers from bronchial asthma. It has nothing to do with living with cockroaches, however, or being exposed to lead paint, or smoking cigarettes. Felicia's respiratory illness comes from the contaminated land that she lives on each and every day. At different times of the day, she comes into contact with certain chemical smells, which cause her to have a hard time breathing. She does not have the finances to move to a better neighborhood. The Worleys' apartment complex is built on a superfund—a piece of land that is contaminated due to hazardous waste

being dumped or left out in the open, the effects of which dispropor-
tionally affect African Americans and people living in poverty.[8] The
government, particularly the Environmental Protection Agency (EPA),
is responsible for cleaning up these hazardous waste sites.[9] A few years
ago, the EPA approved a plan for cleaning up the waste site in which
Felicia Worley lives, but the project has yet to begin. The Worleys are
not alone; landfills and hazardous waste sites are found just about everywhere people experiencing poverty live.

Zip code 10567 is an area in which the Ruiz family lived for a few
years. It is also the same zip code of the Magna Metals plant located in
upstate New York from 1955 to 1979. During the operations of the
Magna Metals plant, iron, lead, copper, nickel, zinc, cyanides, and sul-
fates were all discharged into nearby leaching pits.[10] As a result, the
groundwater, soil, and streams were all contaminated with metals and
other volatile hazardous waste.[11] In 2013, the Magna Metals plant was
demolished; at present, there are warehouse buildings, offices, and residential homes being built adjacent to and on the contaminated soil. In
1987, the EPA completed their assessment and determined that this
waste site needed to be cleaned up, but the Magna Metals plant was
only put on the priorities list as of May 2019.[12] What is even more
frightening is that the EPA has not made a statement to the public about
whether the hazardous site has been cleaned up and removed from the
national priorities list. When I spoke with Ferdinand Ruiz, he stated,
"We are not shocked nothing has been done in the area . . . they prom-
ised us that they would clean up the land when we lived here years ago,
but they never did." He added that "there were times that it was so bad
that you could smell the burning of metals and see the black smoke
from miles away." This was not the first time the Ruiz family experienced the effects of pollutants and other hazardous materials. Mercedes
stated, "Back home in Puerto Rico, my aunt had died from the water
being contaminated. It took a while for my family to figure it out, but
we now know it was the training that the United States Department of
Defense was conducting on the island."

From the 1940s until 2003, the US Navy used Vieques, Puerto Rico,
as a military training site.[13] Oftentimes the training exercises consisted

of ship-to-shore gunfire, as well as air-to-ground bombing by naval aircraft. Since the early 2000s, the ammunition fragments from the explosions have not only contaminated the drinking water on the island, but the surrounding beaches as well. A number of hazardous materials have been found at the site from the explosions, such as mercury, lead, copper, magnesium, lithium, and pesticides.[14] While Vieques made the national priorities list for cleanup in 2004, the government still has not yet set a date for when cleanup will be completed or when the site will be safe for reuse and redevelopment. No wonder Vieques is the home of some of the highest sickness rates in the Caribbean. A study done by the University of Puerto Rico Graduate School of Public Health found that people who reside in Vieques are eight times more likely to die of cardiovascular disease and seven times more likely to die of diabetes than other people who live on the island.[15]

I asked Mercedes the question, "What emotion comes to mind when you think about Puerto Rico?" Her response was,

> Pure sadness. . . . My heart goes out to the families that want to get away from the big cities like New York, and Chicago, and come down to enjoy our beautiful beaches with clear blue water. Many of them have low-paying jobs, or work paycheck to paycheck to save their money for years just to take a vacation and come to Puerto Rico, but instead of getting a vacation of a lifetime, it turns out that Puerto Rico gives them some type of chronic illness for the rest of their life from our contaminated drinking water and beaches and they don't have the slightest clue of what is happening in Vieques, Puerto Rico.

She continued, "But what saddens me the most is that the United States Department of Defense has openly admitted that they did use metals and other chemicals such as Agent Orange on the island. However, they denied that there was any link between their military training exercises (bombing) and the health conditions of the people who live in Vieques, Puerto Rico."

In order for the US government to help people in need and provide funding and other forms of relief, it requires some standard of causal evidence that it is solely responsible for the health conditions. The government's policy is that it has to be convinced that it actually did something wrong. Usually, this means an independent investigation would take place in Vieques. But the federal government still controls the land that was occupied by the military. The government has the final say on who has access to the land and who can conduct research to determine how people in Vieques became ill. But if independent scholars cannot conduct research in Vieques, then it is going to be almost impossible to prove that the US government is responsible for the health crisis there.

Policy of Habitability: Harmful to Live with Cockroaches

Many urban neighborhoods have another infamous, uncelebrated environmental hazard—a thriving cockroach infestation. The cockroach has existed for millions of years and will be here long after humans are removed from this earth. The presence of cockroach allergen is extremely problematic in the inner city, where it has been linked to poor asthma outcomes.[16] During the 1950s, in the Carmelitos Public Housing Development located in Los Angeles, California, an outbreak took place where 39% of all asthma cases occurred amongst the people living in the housing project. It wasn't until a full-scale treatment of cockroach insecticide (silica aerogel Dri-Die 67) was implemented that the outbreak came to an end. It was later discovered that the cockroaches traveled back and forth between the sewage system and the housing project.[17] Today, an estimated 26.1% of the US population who live in inner-city neighborhoods exhibits allergic sensitization to the German cockroach, based on positive skin tests from the National Health and Nutrition Examination Survey.[18]

When I met with the Rubio family, they explained what it was like dealing with roach infestations and the delays associated with getting their apartment exterminated by the New York City Housing Authority. When I approached Josephine Rubio's apartment, I saw cockroaches crawling in the stairway outside the front door. When I entered the apartment, there were roaches all over the trash and in the cabinets. To demonstrate how awful the cockroach infestation was in her apartment, Josephine's son Sebastian shook the toaster oven and roaches fell out. Josephine stared at me without saying a word, but it was clear from the look in her eyes that she was embarrassed and needed help. It was evident that Josephine wanted me to know that living with all those roaches was not just a public health problem, but seeing them on the walls, on the kitchen table, and under the table every single day was also a mental health issue.

Pest control efforts in low-income urban neighborhoods are not working. Josephine complained to the New York City Housing Authority in September of 2016 about the roach infestation in her apartment. She stated,

> The Housing Authority had a private contractor come and spray the apartment, but after the contractors left my apartment I kept seeing roaches and the infestation had gotten worse. I called the Public Housing Authority and put in a request that my apartment needed to be sprayed, but I would only receive notices on my apartment door stating they would send someone out to spray my apartment. But no one from the Public Housing Authority ever showed up to exterminate the roaches.

The reason why Josephine was (and is) having difficulty getting her apartment exterminated is because of the local polices that have been implemented by the New York City Housing Authority. Remember, in order for the public housing authority to spray an apartment, Josephine must put in a request for extermination—but this is only one half of the harmful policy. The other half of the policy is that the public housing authority needs to see evidence that there is a cockroach infestation before they can spray chemicals in an apartment. This promotes victim blaming and sends the wrong message. This also allows for the public housing authority to be free of blame when it comes to cockroach infestation in people's apartments.

When I spoke with the Blackmon family, it took Shelia Blackmon 20 minutes to gather her thoughts before she shared the horrific experience of having a roach crawl into her ear in the middle of the night while sleeping in her new apartment complex. She explained that a few months prior to our meeting, she and her husband had moved into their new apartment in New York City. The apartment was newly renovated but had one annoying downside, which was the presence of cockroaches. Shelia and Lester wanted to move out of that apartment complex, but the rent was affordable and they knew it would be difficult finding another place to live that was within their budget. So they decided to tough it out and avoid being put back on a waiting list.

Anyone who has lived in housing projects fully understands the difficulty of trying to rid themselves of roaches. A few days after Lester and Shelia moved into their new apartment, they began using fogging machines to help eliminate the roaches in their apartment. Unfortunately, to their surprise, the roach problem was about to take a turn for the worse. One September evening, Shelia shot out of bed, disoriented, stumbling to the bathroom. She quickly noticed that something was wrong with her right ear. She grabbed a cotton swab and gently put it in her ear, and felt something move. When she pulled the cotton swab out, she saw two dark brown skinny pieces stuck to the cotton swab. Immediately she realized that they were the legs of a cockroach. She began to panic, and her husband immediately ran to the bathroom to see what was happening. He looked into his wife's ear and confirmed that the roach was trying to dig its way further into her ear.

In that moment, her husband was her only hope. He grabbed a pair of tweezers and tried to pull the roach out from its thickest body part, but was unsuccessful. As her husband tried to delicately remove the roach from his wife's ear, she could feel the roach wiggle its way deeper in her ear canal. At that moment, Shelia and Lester panicked and began knocking on their neighbor's door for help. Luckily, an older woman in apartment 2B heard the commotion and came out to help. The woman immediately asked if Shelia was in pain. Shelia replied, "I am not in pain, but I feel as though I am going to vomit." She continued, "The roach crawled in my ear while I was asleep and now it's stuck."

The older woman ran back into her apartment and grabbed some baby oil. She told Shelia to stay calm and lie down with her right ear facing upward. As the woman administered the baby oil to Shelia's ear, the roach began to react and could no longer move deeper into the ear canal, as the baby oil caused the roach to rise toward the outer ear. It took about one minute for the roach to rise toward the opening of the ear. Then, using curved tweezers, the older woman removed the roach and placed it on a napkin. The older woman told Shelia that extracting roaches from someone's ear happened about once a month in those low-income housing units. In fact, Shelia was the second person during the month of September to have a roach removed from their ear canal. Before this incident, the older woman explained, her grandson had to have a roach removed from his ear.

One would think that since Shelia Blackmon is a tenant, she would be protected under the Implied Warranty of Habitability law. The Implied Warranty of Habitability places the onus on the landlord to maintain livable conditions for their tenants and ensure that the tenant's property is protected from common pests. But the Implied Warranty of Habitability is actually harmful to most low-income tenants. When the Implied Warranty of Habitability indicates that the landlord must maintain livable conditions for their tenants, it is referring to natural circumstances. For example, if an apartment building is located next to a grassy field and a tenant reports mice entering their apartment, then the landlord is responsible for arranging to pay and have the mice exterminated from the tenant's residence. But, if the landlord can show that the mouse infestation was somehow associated with the tenant's way of living, behavior, or other actions, then the tenant must pay for and deal with the problem. Shelia wanted to confront her landlord. But she did not think she could convince a judge in court that the cockroaches in her home originated from her apartment building being dirty or the garbage not being taken out regularly. So she did not seek justice.

The lives of people who live in low-income urban neighborhoods are difficult enough without them having to prove that as tenants, their lifestyle did not cause them to have cockroaches in their home. This does not eliminate the other barriers that potentially stand in their way when filing a lawsuit against their landlord. A study conducted by Rutgers Law School found that the Implied Warranty of Habitability can and does work for tenants if it's used. However, because of obstacles such as tenant "blacklisting," the scarcity of effective assistance from lawyers, and tenants' lack of awareness of their basic rights, very seldom would the Implied Warranty of Habitability be used to prevent housing violations.[19]

The stories of Shelia Blackmon and Josephine Rubio resonate with my own personal experience. As a child, I can remember my brother and I staying in my grandmother's public housing apartment and getting up in the middle of the night to get something to drink. Whenever we turned on the kitchen light, we would see roaches scurrying across the kitchen floor and the countertops. Every time I saw roaches in the middle of the night, I could not fall back asleep. I was horrified that roaches would be crawling all over me and particularly in my mouth and ears. As a family, we were always hesitant to admit that we had cockroaches because we were embarrassed of what people would think about our home. Unfortunately, I would learn that that was a mistake, when a few years later my brother died of an asthma attack that may have been directly linked to living in a low-income inner-city neighborhood with cockroaches.

Coronavirus Deaths: Disproportionately Higher Numbers in Certain Zip Codes

While my research for this book preceded the COVID-19 pandemic, there is some information that is worthy of sharing as it relates to health disparities in urban neighborhoods. The COVID-19 pandemic has done something remarkable that very few viruses have done up to this point, which is to reveal that health disparities exist in the wealthiest and most technologically advanced country in the world.

The SARS-CoV-2 coronavirus caused a novel disease that has forced many states to implement a stay-at-home order to reduce the spread of COVID-19. However, statistics show that African Americans are disproportionately being affected by COVID-19, particularly those living in low-income neighborhoods. African Americans are known to have lower-paying jobs compared to their white counterparts, which lessens their chances of having extra money put aside during a crisis such as a global pandemic. Many African Americans cannot afford not to work because they have jobs that pay an hourly wage, such as store clerks or fast-food restaurant workers.[20] Working in these types of establishments puts African Americans on the front lines of the fight against COVID-19, because their jobs are considered to be essential. However, it also puts African Americans at a higher risk of exposure to the coronavirus. We witnessed African Americans practicing social distancing much later than whites, largely because they don't have the luxury to stay at home and work.

In the United States, Blacks have died from COVID-19 at a rate of 50.3 per 100,000, compared to 20.7 for whites. There is evidence that many of the deaths that occurred due to COVID-19 for Blacks are precipitated by underlying health conditions such as diabetes, heart disease, hypertension, and obesity. While these preexisting health conditions are a factor in COVID-19-related deaths, there is mounting evidence that death rates due to the coronavirus are disproportionately higher in certain zip codes. In New York City, when the city health department reported the first couple of deaths by race, it showed that Black New Yorkers, especially those who live in the Bronx and Queens, were experiencing death rates at least twice those of whites and Asians. The underlying issue of why we see so many deaths in certain zip codes where a majority of Black and brown people live is a profound structural inequality.[21]

The Dangers of Using Gas Stoves in Housing Projects

The use of gas stoves and ovens in urban neighborhoods, especially in housing projects, has been linked to chronic bronchitis, impaired lung function, asthma, the exacerbation of allergies, and cardiovascular disease.[22] In 1826, James Sharp created the first gas stove with the idea of people being able to cook food for themselves and their families. Originally, the gas stove—or "baseburner," as it was called—was located outside in the back of the house because it produced large amounts of fumes from burning coal and the stove had to be turned on by lighting a match, which made it very easy to explode.[23]

As gas became an important source of fuel, the manufacturers of gas stoves wanted to bring this energy source into people's homes for millions to be able to access this technology. This was done by installing a pilot light as a safety feature in their gas stoves. This is the clicking noise that you hear when you ignite the stove, which prevents the stove from causing an explosion. However, even when these safety measures were put in place to prevent fires in the home, they still did not eliminate residential carbon monoxide, which is generated from gas stoves and is associated with respiratory infections.[24] Nearly 42% of adults living in the inner city use natural gas stoves for cooking, and 47% use gas to heat their homes and apartments.[25] Over the last century, exposures to poisonous gas have resulted in medical emergencies and major health problems in urban neighborhoods. Residential carbon monoxide from gas stoves is one of the major contributors to death in the United States, killing approximately 450 people annually.[26] Research shows that 73% of the estimated carbon monoxide events seen in emergency departments occur in urban neighborhoods.[27]

A Smoke-Free Workplace: No Safe Level of Secondhand Smoke Exposure

Exposure to tobacco smoke has been a major topic of interest to public health professionals during the twentieth century because of its negative impact on the health of vulnerable populations living in urban neighborhoods. Since the US Surgeon General's report came out in 1964, high numbers of health care professionals have taken the stance—and continue to argue—that there is no safe level of exposure to tobacco smoke and that any exposure to secondhand smoke can cause both immediate and long-term damage to the body.[28]

When I conversed with Rosa Santoya, I learned that Rosa was surrounded by secondhand smoke when she was a young girl. Both her mother and her father smoked, and their friends smoked cigarettes. "As a child on Saturday mornings, I remember Mom lighting up a cigarette before she started cleaning, then she would come back to take a quick puff of the cigarette before she began cleaning the house again," Rosa said.

> I wanted to be just like my mom when I was growing up. . . . One day I stole a cigarette out of my mother's purse and placed it under my bed. When my mother was sleeping, I pulled the cigarette out from under the bed and began pretending I was my mother. I stood in front of the mirror and put the unlit cigarette up to my lips as if I was blowing out smoke. I was copying my mother's every move to perfection. I remember being yelled at by my mom when she noticed that her cigarettes were missing from her purse.

"I don't remember my mom telling me not to play with cigarettes because they could make me sick," Rosa continued. "I do remember being sick and missing school on a number of occasions, especially during the winter months, due to bronchitis and asthma. My little sister and I had to play inside the house with cigarette smoke in the air. I was coughing and hacking up phlegm and I reeked of cigarette smoke."

She added, "I recall the day my mother died of lung cancer because it was the same day that my father decided to quit smoking cigarettes. I still have my mother's favorite ashtray to this day. I keep it because it's a constant reminder of what my mom has given me to live with for the rest of my life, without my knowledge or me agreeing to it, which is a respiratory illness from secondhand smoke."

As a child, I frequently went to the corner store and purchased "loosie cigarettes" (single cigarettes that you could buy for 25 cents if you did not have enough money to purchase a pack) for my uncle and a few of his friends, so that I could keep the spare change to buy myself some candy. It was common in my neighborhood for people to be smoking everywhere. Adults would perform tricks by inhaling the cigarette smoke and making smoke rings come out of their mouth. I would sit on the park bench and watch adults smoke for hours and never complained about the secondhand cigarette smoke blowing in my face, affecting my health. Just like Rosa Santoya, I had no idea I was putting myself at risk of developing bronchitis or asthma from secondhand smoke.

In contrast, the Hughes family were exposed to cigarette smoke by living around people who smoked in their workplace. The Hughes family lives in a split-level private home in the Bronx, where they rent out the bottom half of the house to a single mom who smokes cigarettes and makes a living doing hair out of her home for people who live in the neighborhood. Dave and Regina Hughes occupy the upper level of the home, along with their two sons and two daughters. Their youngest daughter suffers from asthma and has been hospitalized a few times due to the severity of her asthma attacks.

Since 2019, the Hughes family has been complaining to the owner of the house about their exposure to cigarette smoke, which is affecting the health of their youngest daughter. The owner of the home assured the Hughes family that their rights were protected under the comprehensive smoke-free law in the Bronx that prohibited smoking in workplaces, restaurants, and bars.[29] What the landlord failed to realize was that the hairdresser was smoking in their private residence. In fact, a disproportionately high number of African Americans with low incomes who live in urban neighborhoods smoke cigarettes and have service jobs or side hustles out of their homes.[30] For example, a study found that on the west side of Chicago, a significant amount of Black women living in poverty did some hairdressing work on the side, tried to sell Mary Kay cosmetics, and made spaghetti and fish dinners to sell to their friends on the weekend to pay bills and feed their family.[31]

The Hughes family was able to file a lawsuit against the homeowner on the grounds of nuisance. According to the law of nuisance, if someone is acting in a manner that is unreasonable and impacts everyone in the home to the point where they can no longer enjoy the use of their home, they have the right to bring suit.[32] The courts ruled on behalf of the Hughes family on the grounds that the comprehensive smoke-free law prohibits smoking in public places and places of employment.

The comprehensive smoke-free law does not prohibit anyone from smoking in the privacy of their own home unless their private residence is a daycare for children. The hairdresser's apartment is considered to be a residence at all times. However, once the hairdresser began doing hair during normal business hours between 9 a.m. and 5 p.m., she turned her place of residence into her own personal workplace which now prohibits smoking in that apartment. This is the same ruling that the courts upheld in Florida, where a nonsmoker was awarded $1,000 after she argued in court that her condominium neighbor's smoke was trespassing, a nuisance, and violated her right to a clean indoor air environment. The nonsmoking family was harmed by the smoke and had to sleep elsewhere when the dense smoke entered their condominium.[33]

Tobacco-related health disparities in urban neighborhoods are here to stay. Many families with low incomes are often too afraid to challenge the cultural norms in their community. Individuals would rather remain silent than approach their landlord and ask them to tell other tenants not to smoke, because they want to show the other individual (or individuals) that they are friendly and not a "snitch." They are willing to show their respect by not interfering with personal decisions and avoiding confrontation. These cultural values are in every low-income urban neighborhood. However, to not ask your neighbor to change their smoking behavior comes at a cost. The Hughes family had the right mindset by making their voices heard and showing how the law hindered and jeopardized their family's health as opposed to helping them against the dangers of secondhand smoke.

Notes

1. Green and Leon, "Citizen."
2. Green and Leon, "Citizen."
3. Green and Leon, "Citizen."
4. Green and Leon, "Resistance."
5. Mackenzie and Turrentine, "Air Pollution."
6. Initially, King Charles II refused to clean up the air pollution in London until he met John Evelyn, who published the *Fumifugium* in 1661.
7. United Nations Department of Economic and Social Affairs, "World's Population Increasingly Urban."
8. United States Environmental Protection Agency, "What Is Superfund?"
9. On December 2, 1970, the Senate confirmed William Ruckelshaus as the first administrator of the Environmental Protection Agency, which is also the traditional date we currently use as the birth of the EPA. Five months earlier, in

July of 1970, President Richard M. Nixon had signed Reorganization Plan No. 3, calling for the establishment of the EPA.

10. United States Environmental Protection Agency, "Magna Metal Cortlandt Manor, NY."

11. United States Environmental Protection Agency, "Magna Metal Cortlandt Manor, NY."

12. United States Environmental Protection Agency, "Magna Metal Cortlandt Manor, NY."

13. In 1941, Vieques, Puerto Rico, was chosen by the United States government because it was the only place on the East Coast where aircraft, naval surface ships, and ground forces could conduct combined arms training with live ammunition under realistic conditions in a coordinated manner. See United States Environmental Protection Agency, "Atlantic Fleet Weapons Training Area."

14. United States Environmental Protection Agency, "Atlantic Fleet Weapons Training Area."

15. Pelet, "Puerto Rico's Invisible Health Crisis."

16. Cohn et al., "National Prevalence and Exposure Risk."

17. Kreston, "Everything You Didn't Want to Know."

18. The National Health and Nutrition Examination Survey is designed to examine the health and nutritional status of adults and children in the United States. The survey is unique in that it collects data from in-home personal interviews and physical examinations inside mobile lab examination centers.

19. Jenkins, "Amid Push to Replace Natural Gas."

20. Sawani and Malcom, "Racial Disparities in the Time of COVID-19."

21. Pilkington, "Black Americans Dying of Covid-19."

22. Fandiño-Del-Rio et al., "Effects of a Liquefied Petroleum."

23. Petty, "History of Gas Stoves."

24. Petty, "History of Gas Stoves."

25. Jenkins, "Amid Push to Replace Natural Gas."

26. McDonald et al., "Residential Carbon Monoxide (CO) Poisoning Risks."

27. McDonald et al., "Residential Carbon Monoxide (CO) Poisoning Risks."

28. On January 11, 1964, Dr. Luther Terry released the first US Surgeon General's Report on smoking and health, which led to Congress calling for the Federal Cigarette Labeling and Advertising Act of 1965 and the Public Health Cigarette Smoking Act of 1969. These laws required warning labels to be printed on cigarette packets, banned cigarette advertising in the media, and entailed annual reports on the health consequences of cigarette smoking.

29. Campaign for Tobacco Free Kids, "U.S. State and Local Issues."

30. Dugan Adell, "Double Burden of the Black Hustle."

31. Dugan Adell, "Double Burden of the Black Hustle."

32. Lehman and Phelps, West's Encyclopedia of American Law.

33. Merrill v. Bosser, No. 05–4239 COCE 53 (Broward County Ct., June 29, 2005). See NOLO, "When Secondhand Smoke Invades Your Home."

Bibliography

Campaign for Tobacco Free Kids. "U.S. State and Local Issues: Smoke-Free Laws." April 1, 2023. https://www.tobaccofreekids.org/what-we-do/us/smoke-free-laws.

Cohn, Richard D., Samuel J. Arbes Jr., Renee Jaramillo, Laura H. Reid, and Darryl C. Zeldin. "National Prevalence and Exposure Risk for Cockroach Allergen in U.S. Households." *Environmental Health Perspectives* 114, no. 4 (2006): 522–26. https://doi.org/10.1289/ehp.8561.

Dugan Adell, Meegan. "The Double Burden of the Black Hustle." *The Thread* (New America), March 1, 2022. https://www.newamerica.org/the-thread/the-double-burden-of-the-black-hustle/.

Fandiño-Del-Rio, Magdalena, Dina Goodman, Josiah L. Kephart, Catherine H. Miele, Kendra N. Williams, Mitra Moazzami, Elizabeth C. Fung, et al. "Effects of a Liquefied Petroleum Gas Stove Intervention on Pollutant Exposure and Adult Cardiopulmonary Outcomes (CHAP): Study Protocol for a Randomized Controlled Trial." *Trials* 18, no. 1 (2017): 518. https://doi.org/10.1186/s13063-017-2179-x.

Franzese, Paula A., Abbott Gorin, and David J. Guzik. "The Implied Warranty of Habitability Lives: Making Real the Promise of Landlord-Tenant Reform." *Rutgers University Law Review* 69, no. 1 (2016): pp. 1–45. https://www.rutgerslawreview.com/wp-content/uploads/2017/07/Franzese-Gorin-Guzik-The-Implied-Warranty-of-Habitability-Lives-69-Rutgers-UL-Rev-1-2016.pdf.

Green, Reinaldo Marcus, and Kenny Leon, dirs. *Amend: The Fight for America.* Season 1, Episode 1, "Citizen." Aired on February 17, 2021, on Netflix. https://www.netflix.com/ca/title/80219054.

Green, Reinaldo Marcus, and Kenny Leon, dirs. *Amend: The Fight for America.* Season 1, Episode 2, "Resistance." Aired on February 17, 2021, on Netflix. https://www.netflix.com/ca/title/80219054.

Jenkins, Lisa Martine. "Amid Push to Replace Natural Gas, Public Is Split on Whether to Electrify Their Homes." *Morning Consult*, February 12, 2021. https://morningconsult.com/2021/02/12/energy-efficiency-series-natural-gas-electric-alternatives-polling/.

Kreston, Rebecca. "Everything You Didn't Want to Know about Cockroaches." *Discover Magazine*, May 9, 2012. https://www.discovermagazine.com/the-sciences/everything-you-didnt-want-to-know-about-cockroaches.

Lehman, Jeffrey, and Shirelle Phelps. *West's Encyclopedia of American Law.* 2nd ed. Detroit: Gale Publications, 2005.

Mackenzie, Jillian, and Jeff Turrentine. "Air Pollution: Everything You Need to Know." NRDC. Last updated June 22, 2021. https://www.nrdc.org/stories/air-pollution-everything-you-need-know.

McDonald, Eileen M., Andrea C. Gielen, Wendy C. Shields, Rebecca Stepnitz, Elizabeth Parker, Xia Ma, and David Bishai. "Residential Carbon Monoxide

(CO) Poisoning Risks: Correlates of Observed CO Alarm Use in Urban Households." *Journal of Environmental Health* 76, no. 3 (2013): 26–32. https://www.ncbi.nlm.nih.gov/pmc/articles/PMC6413869/.

NOLO. "When Secondhand Smoke Invades Your Home." NOLO. Accessed April 20, 2022. https://www.nolo.com/legal-encyclopedia/when-neighbors -secondhand-smoke-invades-home.html#:~:text=Sue%20Your%20Neighbor, use%20and%20enjoy%20your%20property.

Pelet, Valeria. "Puerto Rico's Invisible Health Crisis." *Atlantic* (New Hampshire, NW), September 3, 2016. https://www.theatlantic.com/politics/archive/2016 /09/vieques-invisible-health-crisis/498428/.

Petty, Marsanne. "History of Gas Stoves." HomeSteady. Updated September 26, 2017. https://homesteady.com/facts-5103941-history-gas-stoves.html.

Pilkington, Ed. "Black Americans Dying of Covid-19 at Three Times the Rate of White People." *Guardian*, May 20, 2020. https://www.theguardian.com/world /2020/may/20/black-americans-death-rate-covid-19-coronavirus.

Sawani, Jina, and Kelly Malcom. "Racial Disparities in the Time of COVID-19." *Michigan Health* (Ann Arbor, MI), May 4, 2020. https://labblog.uofmhealth .org/rounds/racial-disparities-time-of-covid-19.

United Nations Department of Economic and Social Affairs. "World's Population Increasingly Urban with More Than Half Living in Urban Areas." Updated July 10, 2014. https://www.un.org/development/desa/en/news /population/world-urbanization-prospects.html.

United States Environmental Protection Agency. "Atlantic Fleet Weapons Training Area: Vieques, PR." Updated May 13, 2020. https://cumulis.epa.gov /supercpad/SiteProfiles/index.cfm?fuseaction=second.schedule&id=0204694.

United States Environmental Protection Agency. "Magna Metal Cortlandt Manor, NY." Last updated April 6, 2022. https://cumulis.epa.gov/supercpad /SiteProfiles/index.cfm?fuseaction=second.cleanup&id=0201321.

United States Environmental Protection Agency. "What Is Superfund?" Last updated November 19, 2021. https://www.epa.gov/superfund/what-superfund.

THREE

Oral Health in Low-Income Neighborhoods

"I am not obligated to treat you"

MANY OF THE friends that I grew up with in Edenwald Houses would play the "dozens game." We would put each other down by talking about each other's clothes, sneakers, haircuts, or grills (mouths). It did not matter if you could not afford to purchase the latest style of clothing or owned a pair of Adidas sneakers with the fat shoestring laces in them. You were guaranteed to come out on top and have the joke of the night if your teeth were pearly white and your friend's teeth were yellow and they had halitosis (bad breath).

There was a time when we smiled with our teeth showing. Today, we acknowledge one another with a simple nod of the head and a "fake smile" without showing our teeth. Even when we find something extremely funny, we laugh and cover our mouths because we are embarrassed to show our teeth. The lack of dental services in low-income neighborhoods has resulted in high levels of cavities and gum disease.[1]

My oral health in the 1980s was far different from my oral health today. Growing up, we only had one type of toothpaste: Arm & Hammer baking soda. Back then toothpaste was used for whitening teeth. Today, toothpaste freshens our breath, cleans gums, and strengthens enamel. Back then, we brushed our teeth with a flat toothbrush. When we did not have a toothbrush, we used our finger and put toothpaste on it to brush our teeth. My mother would tell my siblings and I to roll the toothpaste from the bottom of the tube because the toothpaste had to last for several weeks.

We always had toothpaste, but we did not have dental floss. We cleaned food from between our teeth throughout the day with different-colored toothpicks that my mom purchased from the local Woolworths. After dinner, I would use my grandmother's home remedy, which consisted of one teaspoon of salt and two teaspoons of baking soda placed on a dampened toothbrush. In the mid-1980s, we started using the original formula of Listerine mouthwash. I remember this vividly because when I first gargled the mouthwash, I felt a slight burning sensation in my mouth. You either endured the burning sensation of the alcohol, or you did not use mouthwash at all.

When I compare my childhood memories of my oral health with the experience of the Hughes family today, I am flabbergasted to see how much oral hygiene has changed. In contrast to my family having one type of toothpaste, the Hughes family has multiple packs of toothpaste in their home. Every individual has his or her own brand of toothpaste. Dave enjoys using Crest Gum Detoxify, while Regina prefers to use Sensodyne. Their oldest daughter Samantha uses Colgate Ultrabrite Advanced Whitening, and Latasha uses Colgate 2-in-1 whitening toothpaste and mouthwash. Their son Brandon enjoys using Aquafresh, while Thomas prefers to use AIM.

In the Hughes household, their bathroom contains a variety of oral hygiene products, including a Philips Sonicare toothbrush with silicone bristles, stain-dissolving whitening strips, and an oral rinse which happens to be sugar- and gluten-free. Dave and Regina both have what look to me like high-tech water picks, but they never use them—and they have a lot of dental floss.

Brandon loves to eat several meals throughout the day, but never flosses his teeth. Samantha spends hours in the bathroom getting ready for school, but sometimes doesn't brush her teeth because she is in a rush to catch the city bus for school, so she only gargles with mouthwash before heading out the door. Everyone enjoys eating sugary snacks late at night, and sometimes they go to bed without brushing their teeth.

The Ruizes' apartment is quite different. Their bathroom reflects their Puerto Rican heritage. Mercedes Ruiz has a small Puerto Rican flag on the wall opposite her toilet in her bathroom, and a bottle of Colgate Savacol antiseptic mouthwash and a tube of Marvis Aquatic Mint toothpaste under her bathroom sink. Mercedes loves to buy American products but refuses to buy American toothpaste that contains fluoride, even though she is aware it helps prevent cavities.

The Worleys' household was the most devastating to observe, as their socioeconomic status was very much below that of the average family living in an urban housing project. Frank Worley did all he could to provide a basic standard of oral care for his family. Conditions in the bathroom were horrible: the family had to use bottled water to brush their teeth because the water that came out of the bathroom faucet was brown in color from the copper pipes. They each had their own toothbrush, but the bristles were worn down flat on the head of the toothbrush. The family did not own any dental floss or mouthwash. When I first visited the home, there was no toothpaste. The family used a powdered mix of Arm & Hammer baking soda to brush their teeth.

In Dover, Delaware, the Colemans had a much different bathroom arrangement. They lived in poverty, but had access to an abundance of oral hygiene products. Cynthia Coleman has an Oral-B rechargeable toothbrush and a Waterpik professional water flosser. With the majority of the residents from the housing projects in Dover living below the poverty level, I wondered how the Coleman family was able to obtain costly oral hygiene products while receiving government assistance or food stamps. However, I then realized that if they needed toothpaste, they would trade for it with someone in the housing development that needed sugar or milk. They had survived living in the housing projects by bartering with other families who were in the same predicament.

The current private practice system of delivering oral health care is failing many Blacks and Hispanics, to the point where we are seeing Blacks and Hispanics seeking dental attention for a toothache rather than for the purpose of prevention and keeping their teeth white and clean. When we combine lack of education, cultural values and beliefs, lack of access to services, weekly earnings below the poverty level, lack of dental coverage, inaccurate oral health knowledge, and inaccessibility to health professionals of the same ethnicity or race, we get the worst oral health that affects the most vulnerable citizens, including members of racial and ethnic minority groups that live in urban neighborhoods. These barriers to needed dental care are demonstrated by the following:

- In Maryland, a 12-year-old African American boy was in need of a simple $80 tooth extraction. His mother was not insured. Medicaid dentists were difficult to find and their family had lost their Medicaid coverage. The African American boy never did receive his simple procedure. The abscess from the tooth infected his brain. After six weeks in the hospital and two operations, the African American boy died from a toothache.[2]
- A young man's wisdom tooth was hurting. He went to the emergency room, where he received antibiotics and pain medication. He could not afford the medication because he was unemployed and had no access to dental care. The 24-year-old Cincinnati father died after bacteria from the untreated tooth infection caused his brain to swell.[3]
- In Colorado, a 40-year-old man developed a severe toothache to the point where he couldn't eat on one side of his mouth, and he could not find a dentist. He had to put his name in a lottery to be seen by a dentist and was skipped three times. He is having trouble finding a dentist because Medicaid pays too little to its dentists compared to what they can get from private insurance.[4]
- In California, a 39-year-old Hispanic woman has spent years not taking care of her teeth. Most of her top teeth are missing, chipped, or decayed from methamphetamine use or fighting. Over the years she has found coverage, but the only service that dentists are willing to offer her is tooth extraction. She fears that if she gets her teeth pulled, it will get in the way of her advancing out of poverty because of discrimination.[5]
- In Washington, DC, an African American woman was experiencing pain from a toothache. She asked around, trying to find a

dentist's office that would allow her to be seen. She eventually found a place that told her she needed to call every first Wednesday of the month by 6 a.m. to be placed on the waiting list. She had been calling for six months and finally was told they would let her know when to come in for her visit. She was taking a test at school when the office called. Because she did not answer the phone, they went to the next person on the list. She had to start the process all over again.[6]

No one can deny that certain barriers affect access to oral health care within minority populations, especially those people who live in low-income urban neighborhoods. In 2017, researchers found that more than 53 million people lived in areas (particularly poor urban neighborhoods) that the federal government designated as having a lack of dentists.[7] The Health Resources and Services Administration has projected that by 2025, there will be a shortage of dentists in low-income urban neighborhoods, even when the number of new dentists in the workforce are factored in.[8] Perhaps more importantly, in 2013, many African Americans and Hispanics who lived in urban neighborhoods did not have access to a dentist because two-thirds of the dentists in those communities refused to accept Medicaid and other forms of public assistance.[9]

When I spoke with Sabrina Whittredge, she explained that if it had not been for her niece, Phoebe, who had graduated from college with a master's degree in social work, she never would have been able to navigate the Medicaid system for her disabled husband. A few years back, Calvin Whittredge needed to have his tooth extracted because of an infection. Sabrina explained that her constant stress and frustration began not when her husband first had his tooth extracted, but several months before, when she interacted with the Medicaid system for the first time. Her struggles centered on the bureaucratic hurdles that she had to endure and the scarcity of dentists, primarily oral surgeons, who could perform the necessary surgery of extracting her husband's tooth. Both Calvin and Sabrina had to put up with delays, computer glitches, and a lot of driving to appointments before Calvin's procedure was performed. Sabrina stated, "It took five doctors, five health care facilities, eight months, and many miles of driving in the city of Cincinnati, Ohio, before my disabled husband had his infected tooth extracted." She then added, "I could not imagine what it would have been like if Phoebe was not here to help us navigate the Medicaid system."

Calvin and Sabrina Whittredge are just one family who happens to be poor—what about the millions of other families out there struggling to find oral health care in this complex health care system? Not everyone is lucky enough or blessed to have a niece, nephew, or friend to help them navigate the system.

One member of the Rubio family feels that those dentists who refuse to accept Medicaid patients are only adding to the dental access problem, not solving it. Josephine Rubio stated, "A serious part of the problem is that most dentists don't come from low-income neighborhoods like myself and my friends. They come from middle-class families and upper-middle-class families and they make a boatload of money." She went on:

> When patients come into their dentist's office, they think everything is fine because their patients are receiving oral care. They don't see me, or the Latinos out here that look like me. I don't have private dental insurance, and even with my Medicaid card, I may still not have access to a dentist. . . . But it's not their fault, I cannot say it's 100 percent their fault, but they must take some responsibility, especially when they were told about the problem for years. There is all sorts of information out there that tells us that access to dental care for Medicaid patients is a problem.

For a dentist to limit the number of their patients on government assistance or refuse to accept Medicaid patients, just because dentists receive low Medicaid reimbursements, is not a long-term solution for oral health care needs.[10]

In the late 2000s, when the Ruiz family first came to the United States, they endured a number of oral health barriers. Even though the family brushed their teeth at least once daily, they were never given proper brushing and flossing instructions. Some family members went as far as to use a toothpick for interdental cleaning. They often complained that there was a lack of oral health professionals that practiced dentistry in their neighborhood. In many cases, there were no dentists of the same ethnicity as the Ruiz family. The Ruiz family also stated that their greatest barrier was language. Very few dentists and dental hygienists spoke Spanish in the urban neighborhood in which the Ruiz family lived. This barrier made it difficult for the Ruiz family to maneuver through the health care system and nearly impossible to establish an ongoing health care relationship with a dentist or dental hygienist.

"No Duty" or "No Duty to Treat" Policy

This book owes a great deal to Dr. Elizabeth Tobin-Tyler and Dr. Joel B. Teitelbaum, the authors of *Essentials of Health Justice: A Primer*. In their groundbreaking work, they lay out the most basic tenets of US health law.[11] They describe in detail how in the United States, health equity is not a new problem that is developing or one that requires a multinational response.[12] They argue that it is a current problem of our own making, and one that can be solved by ourselves.[13] One of the purposes of *Disparities in Urban Health: The Wounds of Policies and Legal Doctrines* is to build on Dr. Tobin-Tyler and Dr. Teitelbaum's significant work. Another purpose of this book is to connect with the families that have been impacted by policies—something that Dr. Tobin-Tyler and Dr. Teitelbaum did not do.

To fully comprehend the barriers and lack of access to oral health care that the Ruiz family has experienced, we must first look at the early legal health policies that were put in place to make it impossible for people of color experiencing poverty to have good oral health. Nowhere in the US Constitution does it state that health care is a fundamental right. In fact, people have no legal right to health care services or health insurance. Therefore, dentists and dental hygienists have no legal obligation to provide oral health care upon request. This legal doctrine is known as the "no duty" or "no duty to treat" policy. In the 1901 case of *Hurley v. Eddingfield,* the Indiana Supreme Court was asked to rule on the actions of Dr. Eddingfield, who without any reason whatsoever refused to render medical attention, which resulted in the death of a pregnant woman named Charlotte Burk. After deliberating whether or not Dr. Eddingfield had a legal relationship with Mrs. Burk to warrant a duty to treat, the court quoted Indiana's medical licensing act:

> The act regulating the practice of medicine provides for . . . standards of qualification . . . licenses for those found qualified, and penalties for those practicing without a license. The (state licensing) act 1899, p247 is a preventative act, not a compulsive measure. In obtaining the state's license (permission) to practice medicine, the state does not require, and the license does not engage, that he will practice at all or on other terms than he may choose to accept.[14]

To simplify matters, according to the court, Dr. Eddingfield's medical license did not require him to have an obligation to provide health care services. In fact, Indiana's licensing requirement allowed Dr. Eddingfield to have the choice to decide if he wanted to use his skills and acquired knowledge to provide an individual medical service. When we take a closer look at the "no duty" or "no duty to treat" policy, we begin to see that medical licenses are merely a form of quality control— they have nothing to do with gaining access to services.[15] They serve an equivalent function to our driver's licenses. In no way, shape, or form are you required to take an automobile for a drive; the purpose of your driver's license is that should you choose to drive your car from point A to point B, you are permitted to do just that. In the case of Dr. Eddingfield, his medical license did not grant Charlotte Burk access to his services. Similarly, the lack of services from a licensed dentist did not guarantee the Ruiz family oral health services.[16]

Over the years, I have presented my research in major urban cities in the United States, in San Juan, Puerto Rico, and internationally in Toronto, Canada. My goal has always been the same: to explain how the "no duty" or "no duty to treat" policy allows for dentists, clinicians, and other health professionals to rid themselves of the legal responsibility to provide health care upon request. Every time I am invited to a national conference to sit on a panel with experts in the field and present my research, I am always met with some resistance. They remind me that both Medicaid and Medicare give individuals the legal right to not only receive health care services but also receive health care benefits upon request. Therefore, this undermines the argument about the "no duty" or "no duty to treat" policy: there *are* cases wherein a dentist, doctor, or health professional must provide health care upon request. But these services are carried out by a health professional *only* if he or she *chooses* to participate in Medicaid and Medicare. To extend the analogy of a medical license and a driver's license, when a health care provider is choosing not to participate in Medicaid and Medicare, essentially they are choosing what type of cars they don't want to drive.

When we peel back the layers of the "no duty" or "no duty to treat" policy, we see that people who live in urban neighborhoods have access to a dentist if:

1. They have the financial means to pay for oral health care services in full with their own money or through borrowing money from their family and friends;
2. They have the financial means to pay for a low-cost private dental insurance plan that takes care of preventative services (usually two exams, two cleanings, and two X-rays per year);
3. They meet the criteria and are singled out by a dental insurance plan on the basis of a medical condition (individuals with autism and other special needs), age, or income (200% of the federal poverty level or less than $40,840 for a family of three); or,
4. They are fortunate to have a dentist who has been on the front lines battling tooth decay in urban neighborhoods and is willing to make a moral decision to provide free dental services (similar to Dentists without Borders) to people who are in desperate need.[17]

The enormous gap in oral health disparities occurs primarily because of lack of access to dental care services.

In Lester and Shelia's neighborhood, not a day goes by that the Blackmons do not see someone with a missing tooth. Lester and Shelia explained that many people in their neighborhood, especially the adults, have no teeth in their mouth. Shelia has seen her neighbors bring food out of their apartment complex, sit on the front stoop, and struggle to eat a piece of meat properly. She explained that one of her closest friends, who lives two doors down, purposely isolates herself from people in the neighborhood. Shelia stated, "She calls me and I will come over and sit with her for a few hours and then go back home." Having no teeth has affected her neighbor's self-esteem to the point that she will not go on a job interview or attend any block parties or social gatherings in the community.

On the other hand, if you take the subway train a few stops to the North Bronx, to the neighborhood of Riverdale, you will witness a totally different picture. Riverdale has many historic mansions and an amazing view of the Hudson River.[18] Every time Shelia rides through Riverdale, she wonders if she is still in the Bronx. Shelia regularly takes the train to Riverdale to watch her grandson play sports. "Everyone who lives in Riverdale has nice-looking white teeth. In fact, I have never seen anyone in Riverdale with bad-looking teeth. I've seen people with braces, but that is just another way of letting you know that they want excellent straight teeth," Shelia said, adding, "The difference between the people in my neighborhood and the people in Riverdale is that the dentist in Riverdale doesn't take Medicaid patients, no matter how old they are or how much they need the care."

The Ruiz family worries about the future of their oral health. Ferdinand Ruiz remembers being a young teenager and witnessing his grandfather extracting infected teeth using a pliers and twine—without the use of anesthesia—for people in their neighborhood.

Urban neighborhoods are filled with millions of people who do not have access to dental care services. The "no duty" or "no duty to treat" policy continues to influence the nation's health in disproportionate ways. There are organizations such as the Robert Wood Johnson Foundation that are committed to reducing oral health disparities in low-income urban neighborhoods by improving access and quality of care in ways that matter to people living in urban neighborhoods.[19] Unfortunately, at the current rate of progress, it appears that this goal is far out of reach.

Notes

1. Koppelman and Singer-Cohen, "A Workforce Strategy."
2. Gallagher, "Death from a Toothache."
3. Gann, "Man Dies from Toothache."
4. Galewitz, "Medicaid Patients Struggle."
5. Tobias and Bee, "How Bad Teeth."
6. Pollack, "'I can't chew.'"
7. Koppelman and Singer-Cohen, "A Workforce Strategy."
8. US Department of Health and Human Services, Health Resources and Services Administration, National Center for Health Workforce Analysis, "National and State-Level Projections of Dentists and Dental Hygienists in the U.S., 2012–2025."
9. US Department of Health and Human Services, Health Resources and Services Administration, National Center for Health Workforce Analysis, "National and State-Level Projections of Dentists and Dental Hygienists in the U.S., 2012–2025."
10. Galewitz, "Medicaid Patients Struggle."
11. Tobin-Tyler and Teitelbaum, *Essentials of Health Justice*, 4–6.
12. Tobin-Tyler and Teitelbaum, *Essentials of Health Justice*, ix.
13. Tobin-Tyler and Teitelbaum, *Essentials of Health Justice*, ix.
14. Hurley v. Eddingfield, 156 Ind. 416, 59 N.E. 1058 (Ind. 1901), https://www.lexisnexis.com/community/casebrief/p/casebrief-hurley-v-eddingfield.
15. Tobin-Tyler and Teitelbaum, *Essentials of Health Justice*, ix.
16. Tobin-Tyler and Teitelbaum, *Essentials of Health Justice*, 4–6.
17. Tobin-Tyler and Teitelbaum, *Essentials of Health Justice*, 4–6.
18. Nonko, "5 Best Bronx Neighborhoods."
19. Schlotthauer et al., "Evaluating Interventions."

Bibliography

Galewitz, Phil. "Medicaid Patients Struggle to Get Dental Care." *USA Today.* February 15, 2015. https://www.usatoday.com/story/news/2015/02/15/medicaid-patients-struggle-to-get-dental-care/23315811/.

Gallagher, Mehgan. "Death from a Toothache: The Story of Deamonte Driver and Where We Stand Today in Ensuring Access to Dental Health Care for Children in the District." *O'Neil Institute for National and Global Health Law.* March 9, 2018. https://oneill.law.georgetown.edu/death-from-a-toothache-the-story-of-deamonte-driver-and-where-we-stand-today-in-ensuring-access-to-dental-health-care-for-children-in-the-district/.

Gann, Carrie. "Man Dies from Toothache, Couldn't Afford Meds." *ABC News Medical Unit.* September 2, 2011. https://abcnews.go.com/Health/insurance-24-year-dies-toothache/story?id=14438171.

Koppelman, Jane, and Rebecca Singer-Cohen. "A Workforce Strategy for
    Reducing Oral Health Disparities: Dental Therapists." *American Journal of
    Public Health* 107, suppl. 1 (2017): S13–S17. https://doi.org/10.2105/AJPH
    .2017.303747.

Nonko, Emily. "The 5 Best Bronx Neighborhoods to Check Out in 2018." *Brick
    Underground*. August 21, 2018. https://www.brickunderground.com/buy
    /bronx-neighborhoods-2018-best.

Pollack, Harold. "'I can't chew, you know, because the teeth are very weak.'"
    Washington Post. May 8, 2013. https://www.washingtonpost.com/news/wonk
    /wp/2013/05/08/i-cant-chew-you-know-because-the-teeth-are-very-weak/.

Schlotthauer, Amy E., Amy Badler, Scott C. Cook, Debra J. Pérez, and Mar-
    shall H. Chin. "Evaluating Interventions to Reduce Health Care Disparities:
    An RWJF Program." *Health Affairs (Project Hope)* 27, no. 2 (2008): 568–73.
    https://doi.org/10.1377/hlthaff.27.2.568.

Tobias, Manuela, and Fresno Bee. "How Bad Teeth and Lack of Dental Care
    Can Lead to Poverty and Discrimination." *The Californian*. October 22,
    2019. https://www.thecalifornian.com/story/news/2019/10/22/how-bad-teeth
    -and-lack-dental-care-can-lead-poverty-discrimination-california/4065059002/.

Tobin-Tyler, Elizabeth, and Joel B. Teitelbaum. *Essentials of Health Justice: A
    Primer*. 1st ed. Burlington, MA: Jones and Bartlett Learning, 2019.

US Department of Health and Human Services, Health Resources and Services
    Administration, National Center for Health Workforce Analysis. "National
    and State-Level Projections of Dentists and Dental Hygienists in the U.S.,
    2012–2025." Accessed October 6, 2019. https://bhw.hrsa.gov/sites/default/files
    /bureau-health-workforce/data-research/national-state-level-projections
    -dentists.pdf.

[FOUR]

The Connection between Poor Health and Urban Neighborhoods

U PON GRADUATING from college in 1993 I entered the world as a young community health educator focused on eliminating health disparities and inequities in urban areas. While living in New York City, from 1993 to 1995, I witnessed a great deal of poverty in East-chester, Bronx, and in the South Bronx. I saw food insecurity, firearm violence, and homelessness. When I worked and lived in Birmingham, Alabama, from 1998 to 2001, I saw a different kind of poverty.

Unemployment was a common theme in both urban cities, but the consequences seemed much harsher in Birmingham because of blatant systemic racism and discrimination. I grew up in a housing project similar to the ones I visited in Birmingham. The fact that I grew up around drug dealers, hustlers, robbers, and with one of my closest friends working as a pimp, allowed me to be comfortable in these spaces. People who live in low-income urban neighborhoods have no problem testing your toughness to see if you are a punk or one of them. Once they realize that you are one of them and willing to fight to protect what's yours, by any means necessary, they are open to sharing with you—an outsider—if you demonstrate a genuine interest in their world, as long as you're not a snitch.

When I lived in Birmingham, I would visit the urban neighborhood of Bessemer. The housing projects were one story high and made of brick. They had space heaters in many of the apartments because often times the heating unit would not work. There were thousands of African Americans living in a small four-block radius. The average person would wonder: how do all these people live packed in this small urban housing development?

If I ever needed anything, the people would always go out of their way to find a person who was selling that particular item and get them for me so I could purchase it. Many of the guys who stood outside on the front stoop would always offer me a free haircut or shape-up (a trim that cuts along the edges of a natural hairline to straighten it). I always declined their offers because I knew that cutting hair was their side hustle—for those who wanted to make an honest living—and in some cases their only source of income, which allowed them to survive in their neighborhoods. There were many times I had a mini-Afro when I was in Alabama.

When I returned to New York City during the holidays or the summertime, many of my childhood friends would laugh at me and ask, "What happened to your hair and why is it so nappy? You look like a runaway slave . . . man, we need to get you back on point and get you straight to the barbershop." They suggested that I let them hook me up and get me back to normal.

Visiting neighborhoods where people lived in hardship and distress was not easy to deal with on a daily basis. I met single mothers who sometimes did not have food to feed their children. When speaking with Josephine Rubio, it was clear during our interview that she had fallen upon some hard times. She told me,

> I pray every night for God to help me and my kids. It's hard being a single parent and having to be the sole financial provider for my children. Some days we had to go without food to eat because we did not have money to buy groceries. . . . There were times I had to send them to school hungry and tell them to make sure they ate breakfast and lunch at school because I knew that there was no food in the house to feed them when they came back home from school.

I met fathers who were unemployed because they had a criminal record. Rosa Santoya's boyfriend, Ramon Ortiz, who served some time in prison, expressed his frustration about being unemployed:

Ever since I came home from prison, I have not been able to find work. People always say that when you come out of prison that you have paid your debt to society and that you deserve a second chance. But these are the same people who never offer you a job. . . . I've been on several job interviews in the past month, but I always get the same response. We will read your application and then we gonna give you a call. Yet they never do. . . . It's not about the money, don't get it twisted—I need the money to help out my girlfriend with the bills, but I also need some health insurance. I have not been able to take care of my health when I was in prison and so now that I'm out of prison, I want to be healthy, but it takes me having a job so I can be seen by a doctor.

I met grandmothers who had to raise their grandchildren because either one or both of the child's parents were incarcerated or on drugs. Eloise Stevenson explained how she is mentally, emotionally, and financially exhausted from raising her two grandsons:

There are days that I want to crawl under a rock and never come out. Don't get me wrong, I love Ishmael and Elijah, they are the only grandchildren that I have and they are my world. But children should never have to go without their parents being there for them during their teenage years. Every time my son tells me he is going to get some help for his drug addiction, he never does. I can't take the stress anymore and I'm getting sick and tired of being sick and tired—I have high blood pressure, a bad heart, and I suffer from anxiety. At my age, I should be relaxing and enjoying my time on this earth, and not worrying if I will get a phone call from the police telling me my son died of a drug overdose. I don't have a lot of money and my family does not come from money, so if things continue like they have been the past several months, it's going to be difficult for me financially to raise my two grandsons and pay for my high blood pressure and heart disease medication from the pharmacy.

Back then, I did not understand their health outcomes as well as I do today. Although there was a shortage of opportunities for people who lived in this neighborhood, many of them appeared to be healthy and living good lives filled with music, laughter, affection, and love. Over time, I learned that many of these people were not as healthy as they claimed to be, but were in fact dying, and in many cases dying years before they reached their life's potential. I could no longer just look at the surface of these people's lives; I had to dig through the weeds and try to understand the connection between poor health and urban neighborhoods.

When I first visited the Worley family in Birmingham, I could see that they were living in poverty, but I did not feel as though they were any worse off than anyone else that I met in their neighborhood. The parents and their three children were obese. Mr. Worley (the father) and two of the three children had type 2 diabetes. The children were exposed to an unhealthy diet at a very young age. Their diet would consist of white bread, deli meats, pasta, white rice, and sugary beverages such as sweet tea and sodas. The majority of African American women that I met in Birmingham were obese. This was a complete culture shock for me. When I attended church services, these women were all well dressed in their Sunday best outfits and rather large hats. But every once in a while, I would hear some women breathing heavily when they moved around the church or went up to the front of the church for prayer.

In 2006, when I went back home to New York City, I visited the Hughes family in the Bronx. It was at that moment that I realized that things were beginning to change. When I saw Dave and Regina Hughes, I noticed that they had both put on some weight over the years. I could see that their youngest son Thomas, who was 13, was becoming overweight. I truly expected to see some of this when I lived in Birmingham, because food is mostly fried and many people drive cars, which limits the amount of physical activity a person performs in a given day.

But New York City was a different story all together. You practically walk everywhere if you live in the city. As a child, I walked long city blocks before I was able to catch a train or bus to my destination. This is how I would complete my cardio workouts, by walking. Living in New York City for most of my childhood years and then coming back as an adult forced me to look at the city differently. What I was beginning to witness was the proportion of people who lived in low-income neighborhoods starting to become overweight or obese. Sabrina Whittredge talked about how her neighborhood was a major influence on her gaining weight over the years. She stated,

> As a child you could find me riding my bike, doing double Dutch with my friends, and playing tag all day long in the park. As a teenager in school I ran track and field, played softball, and was an elite basketball player. I was very active during my younger years, even though I don't look it today. Life was pretty simple and then I learned that on every street corner was a fast-food restaurant. I would never eat breakfast, but by 11 a.m. I would eat burgers and fries from fast-food restaurants. By 2 p.m., I would be eating chicken and buttermilk biscuits from fast-food restaurants. But the real culprit for my weight gain was the 24-hour gas stations and the corner stores in my neighborhood that were open all day and all night. At midnight I would have cookies and ice cream and all types of sugary snacks if I wanted it from the corner store because of the availability. I truly don't see the culture of our corner stores changing anytime soon. They are open 24 hours a day just so they can make money and sell snacks. They did it when I was a kid and they will continue to do it for generations to come.

The Ruiz family migrated from Vieques, Puerto Rico, to the Bronx in the late 2000s after Sila María Calderón became the governor of Puerto Rico.[1] They came during a time when former President George W. Bush was conducting Navy bombing exercises in Puerto Rico, and it was estimated that the cleanup of the island would take several decades before life was back to normal. Today, the Ruiz family eats an unhealthy diet. Both Ferdinand and Mercedes eat foods high in salt. Ferdinand's doctor has diagnosed him with hypertension (high blood pressure) and told him several times to stop eating foods such as *bacalao* (a type of fish stew) and *pernil* (roast pork), both of which are traditional dishes in Puerto Rico and contain large amounts of sodium. It's possible that Ferdinand will develop kidney disease, heart disease, or eye disease over the next several years due to the complications associated with hypertension.

To complicate matters even further is the story that Ferdinand shared about La Llorona. Traditionally, La Llorona is a popular myth that dates back hundreds of years, where a woman named Maria drowns her two children and begins crying out because of guilt. Allegedly, Maria commits suicide; upon arriving at the gates of heaven, she is denied and sent back to Earth to find her two children. While there are different versions of the story, the folklore usually ends with the ghost of Maria (now known as La Llorona: "the crying woman") floating over bodies of water, weeping, and kidnapping children.[2]

I think it's important to point out that the myth and bedtime story of La Llorona varies depending on who is telling the story. In the case of Ferdinand, he describes what he believes led him to develop hypertension in the first place. Ferdinand stated, "When I lived in Puerto Rico, La Llorona once visited me." Based on Ferdinand's recounting, the tale of La Llorona depicts her as a temptress that lures young men into the jungle after they have been engaging in negative health behaviors, particularly consuming too much alcohol while at the bars. Once these young men follow La Llorona deep into the forest, she lets out a deafening siren-like scream that causes her victims to suffer from a debilitating illness. This tradition of drinking alcohol late at night is what Ferdinand believes gave him hypertension.

His doctor told him to lose weight and cut down on the alcohol consumption. Ferdinand's family found this to be very problematic and took offense to the doctor's recommendations. They said it was La Llorona who caused all these health complications back in Puerto Rico; it was not the drinking of alcohol or the food that they ate. Ferdinand's doctor was not culturally competent when it came to understanding the relationship between culture and food consumption. Nor did he have the common sense to seek out a colleague who might be Latina to explain Puerto Rican culture to him. Ferdinand went on to explain how he had to enlighten his doctor and clarify that for many Puerto Ricans, food provides pleasure, comfort, and a sense of security that is always connected to their culture.

This is a difficult and frustrating situation, but it is not specific to the Ruiz family. We often find that people within other ethnic and racial groups, particularly African Americans, have a difficult time achieving a successful behavior change (such as reducing salt intake, quitting smoking, and consuming less alcohol) once they have been diagnosed with hypertension.[3] Sabrina explained how her disabled husband Calvin loves salt. "Every time I'm in the kitchen cooking my husband a meal, he always wants to know if I added salt. I beg for him to cut out the salt, but it's difficult. I try to get him to stop using salt, but he complains that the meals do not taste the same without the salt." When I asked Calvin why he loves salt so much, he stated that "no one has ever given him the proper guidance on how to cut back on eating salt." He added, "For decades as a single man, all I ate was processed foods, pretzels, and potato chips, and as a result developed a cultural addiction to salt." Similarly, when I spoke with Eloise, she explained that over the years she had developed a taste for foods high in salt.

> As a young girl I stood on top of a chair in the kitchen and watched my mother cook her collard greens with bacon and other foods high in salt. So naturally I did what my mother used to do when it came to cooking. I love cheese, bread, ketchup, crackers, and a nice piece of hard crispy bacon from time to time. . . . We never followed any Food and Drug Administration guidelines. We ate foods high in salt because that is what we could afford, period. I guess the reason why I never was successful at changing my eating habits is because I don't know where to start. . . . No one ever sat me down and explained to me how to read food labels correctly, or explained to me what are good and bad foods to eat. In fact, I can count on one hand how many times a doctor has ever asked me how much salt do I consume.

Studies have shown that behavioral risk factors such as smoking, poor diet, and alcohol consumption have been identified as preventable causes of death and illness associated with health disparities.[4] Even though a variety of unhealthy behaviors have been identified as a major public health concern, there has been very little and in some cases no success in implementing effective strategies for behavior changes, particularly in groups who are the most vulnerable and have the highest risk of developing hypertension.[5] In short, Blacks and Hispanics living in poverty have a higher prevalence of hypertension than non-Hispanic whites. They have a more difficult time reducing their blood pressure, unless they are in compliance with their doctor and take their blood pressure medication on a regular basis.[6] This, of course, is more likely due to lack of income and education rather than race. However, we must keep in mind the cultural differences and how difficult they can be to overcome. Eloise talked about what the culture was like in her low-income neighborhood when she was growing up.

> As a person who was raised in the South, it did not matter what type of soul food you were cooking for your family. If your food consisted of large amounts of seasoning salt, you did not complain because it's about having a strong community connection with one another and survival for you and your family. Every Black Southerner adds salt to their food and we never talk about if the salt is going to cause us to have high blood pressure or hypertension. If I came to your house for dinner and there was no seasoning or salt in your food, I would have to take your "Black card" away [*laughing*]. This is part of the Black Southern culture that was handed down to us from our ancestors.

We cannot forget that for people who were enslaved, cooking was about culture, community, and—most importantly—survival. Since the beginning of the transatlantic slave trade, when millions of Africans were transported across the Atlantic Ocean to the United States and the Caribbean, food was the most important part of the process.[7] Slave captors had to scientifically calculate which food was the cheapest, with the least amount of nutrition, that would keep their captives alive until they reached their final destination.

Listening to Eloise explain the culture of the South, I could only think about how her story resonated with my own story. When I lived in the Bronx, New York, with my grandmother, you never heard anyone in the neighborhood talk about high blood pressure or hypertension. Black people commonly cooked foods such as spiced ham, frozen pot pies, processed chicken tenders, pig feet, pork ribs, macaroni and cheese, and collard greens (cooked with ham hocks). In 2010, the rate of hypertension hospitalizations was 1.4 times higher in high-poverty neighborhoods compared to that of low-poverty neighborhoods.[8] In 2016, the rate of hypertension hospitalizations was 3.5 times higher in high-poverty neighborhoods (for example, Central Bronx, East Harlem, Central Harlem, and Hunts Point) compared to that of low-poverty neighborhoods (for example, Upper East Side, Lower Manhattan, Chelsea, and Greenwich Village).[9] What is most frightening about this is how much hypertension in high-poverty neighborhoods has increased in a short period of time. I anticipate that we will continue to see an upward trend in the number of people who have hypertension who live in high-poverty neighborhoods. When I spoke with Lester Blackmon, he agreed that more people would develop hypertension in the years to come because they are uninformed about the problem. He explained just how easy it is for Blacks and Latinos to suffer from hypertension and be completely unaware of the seriousness of their illness.

I will never forget the day my wife told me that my nose was bleeding while I was sitting in my chair watching television, and she said, "You need to go to the emergency room." So I jumped up and went to the hospital. Keep in mind that this was the 1990s and we didn't know much about high blood pressure. I remember the doctor giving me some medication and telling me to take it easy when I got home. I pretty much ignored the problem after I got home from the hospital. I know that in the medical world, doctors and nurses call high blood pressure "the silent killer." I can walk around my neighborhood all day feeling fine, and not even know that my blood pressure is heating up like a pressure cooker. I guess I don't look at high blood pressure as a disease. When I think about diseases, I think about cancer and HIV, diseases that you can readily feel. My biggest problem is that the treatments are so inconsistent. Back in 1999, I was given more than 30 different types of medicine. Why do I need to take over 30 different types of medicine for high blood pressure? It makes me wonder: should I believe this doctor or not? Or are they just giving me this medication in hopes it will be a cure? It never ends—it feels like a never-ending rollercoaster ride at Great Adventures. So what do I do? I shut down. I stop looking for answers because it seems as though I can never find them. Us [Blacks] don't think about our health as often as we should. This is why I say hypertension in poor Black and Hispanic neighborhoods will continue to skyrocket.

When I was growing up, my uncle was the only person who was health-conscious. He never ate pork, because it was high in salt. He worked out constantly, because he wanted to stay in shape and defend himself living in the Bronx if he felt threatened. He avoided drinking grape soda, which was probably every kid's soft drink of choice if you grew up in the ghetto (because of the added sugar), and he maintained a healthy body weight.

My friends also maintained a healthy body weight by not eating sweets and playing outside until the streetlights came on in the evening. That was their curfew. No one had hypertension or developed type 2 diabetes.

However, for Rosa, staying healthy has always been a struggle:

I know I need to lose weight and do a better job at eating right. I like McDonald's, Popeyes, KFC, and Burger King. You name it, I can tell you that I have eaten there on more than one occasion. I used to think that all I needed to do was take my medication and I would be able to handle my type 2 diabetes. Boy, was I wrong—in order for me to keep my blood sugar under control, I also have to eat healthy and work out several times a week. But this is no walk in the park for me; it's a constant battle every single day of my life.

Many of my aunts and uncles, like Rosa, had challenges with their health. One of my aunts had a stroke and was placed in a nursing home because of her long battle with high blood pressure and being over-weight. After her stroke, she went to physical and occupational therapy every day to reduce her high blood pressure and improve her health.

In the 1990s, my work as an epidemiologist intern with the New York State Department of Health took me to poor areas in Albany, New York. I remember seeing Black and Hispanic people out in the neighborhood, complaining about having insomnia, migraines, bouts of sweating, and even chest pains, all of which can be caused by a number of things, in-cluding hypertension. At that time, I was not cognizant of the symp-toms associated with high blood pressure. Our focus at the New York State Department of Health was on teenage pregnancy and sexually transmitted diseases. During that time period, US Surgeon General Dr. Joycelyn Elders delivered speeches about how to reduce teenage pregnancy and how sexually transmitted diseases could be reduced.[10] At a press conference, she stated, "We should do away with the idea and the stigma that masturbation is something that is awful and that teenagers and young adults should not engage in this activity. . . . No teenager or young adult has ever gotten pregnant or contracted a sexu-ally transmitted disease from masturbating." While serving on the Teen-age Pregnancy and Sexually Transmitted Disease Task Force for the New York State Department of Health, I wanted to continue the mis-sion of Dr. Elders, whose goal was to implement sex education in Amer-ican schools across the country to reduce teenage pregnancy and the spread of sexually transmitted diseases. But Dr. Elders, the first ap-pointed African American surgeon general of the United States, was asked to resign from her position in late 1994, by former President Bill Clinton because of negative publicity. Her outspoken views on suggest-ing schools should encourage kids to masturbate did not go over well with many religious groups. Nearly three decades later, Dr. Elders, 89, continues to hold her ground on issues of sex education. In 2021, during an interview Dr. Elders stated, "there are a lot of things that are sensitive subjects, and just because they're sensitive does not mean we should ig-nore them when they are destroying the fabric of this country."[11]

On the other hand, the Coleman family, in Dover, Delaware, 2010, had a variety of health issues. Richard Coleman, who was in his early

The author talks with Dr. Joycelyn Elders (*right*), the first African American surgeon general of the United States, about her vision in 2001. *Source:* Image provided by the author.

fifties and worked odd jobs from time to time, had gained a significant amount of weight and was diagnosed with hypertension. Cynthia Coleman, a school crossing guard, and 16-year-old Pamela were moderately overweight, while 10-year-old Alex was overweight with recently diagnosed type 2 diabetes.

The families above—the Worleys, the Hugheses, the Blackmons, the Ruizes, the Colemans—provide a snapshot of the many people living in poverty who reside in urban neighborhoods. Over the past decade, poverty has increased across the United States. The number of people living in high-poverty neighborhoods has doubled. In 2000 there were 7.2 million, but today there are currently 13.8 million.[12] These high-poverty neighborhoods are only the tip of the iceberg. When we look further, we see an increase from 2.4% to 4.4% of Americans living in extremely low-income neighborhoods.[13]

My research over the years, along with other scholars in the discipline, has shown associations between negative health outcomes and poverty. We have adequate data to show that controlling one's weight and reducing obesity is extremely difficult when people lack resources, such as money to pay for healthy food and insurance that gives them access to quality health care. Nearly one-third of children in the United States are overweight or obese, which ultimately contributes to negative health consequences.[14] Sadly, these children are more likely to live in high-poverty neighborhoods than adults. One of the most useful studies conducted by the National Survey of Children's Health looked at children from 1971 to 2008.[15] The study revealed that the percentage of children who were overweight was below 10% in 1971 and increased to more than 30% in 2008.[16] Researchers found that socioeconomic status was a risk factor for being overweight, one that includes having limited access to nutrition and a low-calorie diet, environmental conditions in neighborhoods that do not provide sufficient and safe opportunities for exercise, and high levels of sedentary behaviors, such as watching TV.[17] This alarming increase reveals that childhood overweight and obesity in the United States is a complex condition and has not been effectively prevented or managed.[18]

Middle- and upper-classes have greater access to resources necessary for good health.[19] Moreover, people living in poverty have higher rates of diabetes, hypertension, and food insecurity.[20] In one study, which analyzed the association between socioeconomic status and people's food choices and food habits, researchers found that people who have less money are more likely to purchase food that is cheaper and high in fat and sugar. In addition, when participants were asked the question, "In the last twelve months, were there any times that you couldn't afford food, or afford to buy more food, or ran out of food?," the results showed higher rates of food insecurity among African Americans and Hispanics in low-income urban neighborhoods.[21]

Poverty: Treated Differently Under the Constitution

In short, the connection between poor health and urban neighborhoods is poverty. How has the government allowed poverty to become the common denominator between poor health and urban neighborhoods? All of my research has been in search of an answer to this question.

Under the Constitution, poverty is treated differently compared to other characteristics that have been discriminated against, such as race, ethnicity, religion, and gender. The Supreme Court of the United States made a federal mandate stating that if a group of people have similar characteristics (race, ethnicity, religion, and gender), then that group of people has the right to special protections since they have suffered historical trauma and experienced discrimination at the hands of their own government in the past. This is known as the Equal Protection Clause.[22] However, the Supreme Court has never ruled that people who live in poverty are worthy of the same protection in the Constitution under the Equal Protection Clause. The reason for this is invisibility. In cities across this great nation, there are people sleeping under bridges, on park benches, in subway stations, and in tents in areas known as skid rows. Because many people living in poverty are forced to hide, society tells us that they simply don't exist.

People who are impoverished in our society are suppressed; their identity is often taken away, and they are labeled as outcasts or criminals. Writer and poet Adrienne Rich once stated, "When someone describes the world and you are not in it, there is a moment of psychic disequilibrium where you look in the mirror and see absolutely nothing." Many people living in low-income neighborhoods feel this exact way about themselves and the people in their community.[23] American society has decided that people who are poor have no fundamental rights to the most basic necessities in life.

Dr. King's Legacy: Protecting the Health of the Impoverished

"Of all the forms of inequality, injustice in health care is the most shocking and inhumane." These famous words, attributed to Dr. Martin Luther King Jr., give scholars, professors, practitioners, and activists the motivation to keep Dr. King's legacy alive by doing the work of addressing health equity. However, they are not the exact words Dr. King spoke over half a century ago.[24]

In 1966, during a medical committee meeting for human rights at the University of Chicago, Dr. King, who at the time was head of the Southern Christian Leadership Conference, stated, "We are concerned about the constant use of federal funds to support this most notorious expression of segregation. Of all the forms of inequality, injustice in health is the most shocking and inhuman because it often results in physical death," and "I see no alternative to direct action and creative nonviolence to raise the conscience of the nation." If we look at the words used in the second quote, they are very different from the famous words found in the first quote that scholars tend to mention in their publications and speeches.[25]

First, Dr. King spoke of injustice in "health," not health care. Because he was assassinated, we will never know if Dr. King deliberately meant health, rather than health care. What we do know is that Dr. King was unwavering when it came to speaking out against poverty, inadequate housing, lack of education, racism, and the right to vote. We call these characteristics the social determinants of health, which makes it clear that Dr. King spoke about going beyond just health care. Second, Dr. King said that injustice in health is "inhuman," not "inhumane." There is a significant difference when we define these two terms. "Inhumane" suggests cruelty, a lack of compassion for a person's suffering. "Inhuman" is more extreme, referring to a complete lack of humanity; if someone is inhuman, they are dehumanizing others, seeing them as less than human and believing that they should be treated as such by those in power. Third, the distinction between Dr. King's actual words and the words that are commonly (mis)quoted is important because his actual words explain why health injustice is inhuman. Dr. King asserts that "injustice in health is the most shocking and inhuman because it often results in physical death." He could not have said it any more simply: human beings suffer because of injustice, of which death is one of the most brutal consequences. Finally, this brings us to the last sentence of Dr. King's actual words, where he seeks to "raise the conscience of the nation." This sentence is hardly ever mentioned when people quote Dr. King, and yet it's crucial that we recognize these words, because we have a social responsibility to correct this injustice.[26]

This speech came at a time when Dr. King felt it was time to speak up against the Vietnam War. Imagine for a brief moment that in 1965, a young white boy and a young Negro (I do not endorse using the "N-word"; however, for the time period being discussed, it's important that the word is used in this context) boy are sent 8,000 miles away to fight in a war for freedom in Southeast Asia, only to come back to their home state of Georgia and receive unequal treatment. This was something that Rosa told me about her uncle when he returned home from the Vietnam War. He would tell her, "We go over there and we fight for the land that we grow our food on each and every day, we fight for the water that we drink, we fight for freedom and democracy, to only come back home and be treated like enemies of the state." I can resonate with this story. I was told by elders in the Black community, many of whom served in the Vietnam War. How can one of the richest countries in the world watch Negro boys and white boys get injured during war and have different access to medical treatment when they returned to the US.

Another of Dr. King's famous speeches, "Beyond Vietnam—A Time to Break Silence," took place on April 4, 1964, at New York's Riverside Church. In it, he stated, "A nation that continues year after year to spend more money on military defense than on programs of social uplift is approaching spiritual death." Dr. King asked America to shift from a "thing-oriented" society to a "people society." In particular, he wanted to protect the health of the American people, especially those who are impoverished.[27]

Equal Protection Clause of the Fourteenth Amendment

What the Equal Protection Clause states is that it is illegal to single out a group of people and provide unequal treatment to them. However, states have been known to pass laws that give either advantages or disadvantages to one group of persons, but not the other. What makes the Equal Protection Clause of the Fourteenth Amendment so special is that courts not only have the right to scrutinize laws, but scrutinize laws at different levels.[28] When laws were first created in this country, many were made to intentionally exclude African Americans and other racial and ethnic groups, women, and certain religious groups. The Equal Protection Clause attempts to keep lawmakers honest by allowing the courts to scrutinize those laws that may be prejudiced and corrupted against minority groups who can be considered a "suspect class."[29]

Since courts have the right to scrutinize laws at different levels if those laws are prejudiced against minority groups, then the courts must also decide which groups are considered to be a "suspect class" and worthy of protection under the Equal Protection Clause. Courts do this by asking three plain and simple questions:[30]

1. Has the group in question been historically treated unfairly, or been subject to hostility, violence, prejudice, or stigma?
2. Does the group possess an undeniable or highly visible trait?
3. Is the group generally powerless to protect itself through the political process?

Harris v. McRae

Ever since 1868, when the Equal Protection Clause became law, we have seen laws go under "the most rigid scrutiny" when it comes to treating US citizens differently than non-citizens—laws singling out individuals based on their natural origin, laws that treat men and women differently, laws centering on race-based classifications. So where is the protection for those living in poverty? What efforts have been made to scrutinize the laws that affect them? In an abortion case heard by the court, *Harris v. McRae*, a group of pregnant women experiencing poverty challenged the Hyde Amendment. (The Hyde Amendment prohibits the use of Medicaid funds to pay for abortions except for certain specified circumstances such as endangerment of the mother, and victims of rape or incest.)[31] Action was taken to the federal court to determine whether the denying of public funding for certain medically necessary abortions violated the due process clause of the Fifth Amendment. The due process clause indicates that state governments cannot deny any individual their substantive rights, these rights being life, liberty, or property without due process of the law. The Fifth Amendment prohibits the federal government from discrimination. Ultimately, the court decided that poverty, standing alone, is not a "suspect classification." It does not warrant equal protection under high levels of scrutiny or special treatment.

Maher v. Roe

A second abortion case was *Maher v. Roe*. In the Maher case, Connecticut's Department of Social Services decided to reduce the amount of Medicaid benefits given for first-trimester abortions to only those abortions that are deemed medically necessary.[32] The court stated that under the Equal Protection Clause, just because the state has a policy to pay for the expenses of giving birth to a child, it does not mean the state is obligated to pay for a nontherapeutic abortion for those experiencing poverty, especially when they participate in a Medicaid program.[33] The court further explained that financial need alone does not put a person into a "suspect class" for the purposes of equal protection and scrutiny.

San Antonio v. Rodriguez

In a case called *San Antonio v. Rodriguez*, the Texas Minimum Foundation School Program wanted to fund its public schools primarily through property taxes.[34] The property taxes in Rodriguez's district were much lower than the property taxes in other districts, making the amount of money collected to educate Rodriguez's children significantly less per pupil than that allocated for the education of other children in wealthier districts. The courts decided that "education is not a fundamental right," and therefore the case did not need to be scrutinized under the Equal Protection Clause. They further concluded that (1) the Texas funding program did not discriminate against any definable category of "poor" people, and (2) that Rodriguez (the plaintiff) offered no proof that the Texas school funding system did not provide an adequate education to all of its children no matter which school district they were currently living in.[35] The state of Texas relied on the "adequacy" argument, where the state ensured that a basic education was being provided to each child and that each child was given the basic minimal skills necessary for full participation in the political process.[36]

Suspect Class: No Protection for the Poor

The simple fact that our courts do not recognize those living in poverty as a "suspect class" under the Equal Protection Clause answers the question: where is the protection for those experiencing poverty? There is no protection. People living in poverty are trapped. Additionally, people experiencing poverty lack economic or political leverage to persuade those in political power to end such aggressions. As the abortion and educational laws above indicate, there is a history of discriminating against those living in poverty, or "subordinate populations." Those individuals in political power (who are predominantly white, male, heterosexual, and wealthy) have used the political process and the constitutional framework to their benefit, but have allowed people experiencing poverty to suffer under constitutional doctrines because those same people receive "no scrutiny whatsoever."[37] At a bare minimum, laws that discriminate against and have immense impacts on the lives of people living in poverty should have some level of judiciary scrutiny and uphold the Constitution's commitment to equal protection under the law.[38]

Ferdinand is a perfect example of how poverty has negatively impacted his health. Before his doctor diagnosed him with hypertension, Ferdinand had a few health complications: blurred vision, trouble sleeping, trouble concentrating, and chest pain. In the past several weeks, he had not sent in his prescription to have his medication refilled by the pharmacy. He told me, "I was worried about how much I would have to pay out of my own pocket since I no longer was employed, and I just knew that my old health insurance from my former employer would no longer cover the medication cost."

Shelia's husband Lester talked about how living in poverty has crippled and damaged his health over the course of his life. He states,

> I know for a fact that I will probably not live as long as someone who earns more money than I do. All my life, I worked mostly minimum-wage jobs. Whatever little money I do make, it normally does not last me to the end of the month. I don't have a great education and my worn-down neighborhood that I am currently living in has never been safe. . . . This neighborhood was not safe when I was a kid growing up and it certainly is not safe now, especially after dark. I just don't have the resources. . . . Most people don't understand that when you are Black, Hispanic, and poor in this world, that the majority of the time you will be faced with double jeopardy. The first thing is that you are most likely going to come from a poor family, and if that is not enough, you are going to have to deal with the added burden of living in a poor neighborhood. And it doesn't really matter who you are—you could be male, female, tall, short, fat, ugly, pretty or whatever—both of these things can weigh heavily on a person's health.

Although Lester's story is heartbreaking, it is certainly not unique. Eloise also spoke of her experience growing up in poverty and how the cycle of poverty was too much for her family to break. "Sometimes I feel that when I'm just about to get on my feet and something good is about to happen, a monkey wrench gets thrown into the picture and wipes out everything, just like that. And now, for the past who knows how many years, I've been trying to climb out of this financial hole." Eloise did not just fall into poverty one day; a lot of bad things happened to her. Similarly, many people living in poverty don't just have one problem—they tend to have a number of problems and setbacks in life. Eloise and her two sisters were raised in a low-income urban neighborhood by a single mother. All of the girls, including Eloise, had different fathers who never came around to help out the family. Eloise did not get along with her mother: "I remember when I was 16 years old, I got into a fistfight with my mother and she told me to get out of her house since I did not want to abide by her rules." She remembers staying with friends and sometimes sleeping in the street. "I never went to school—every chance I had, I would drink and smoke. I later became pregnant when I turned 19 by this guy I was seeing, but soon after I had my son, he left me for another girl."

Like many people living in poverty, Eloise began carrying her hardships from childhood into adulthood. "I remember working in grocery stores, packing bags, stocking up shelves with food, mopping the floors, and taking out the trash just so I could have some money in my pocket. There were plenty of times I was hungry and had to stay in a homeless shelter." But what is most disturbing is how poverty has now grabbed hold of her son. Eloise stated, "I used to be in these streets and now my son is in these streets, hooked on drugs and God knows doing what else. He has two boys, with two different women. I hope this is not the legacy I leave behind. I hope my grandchildren can do better than what I did and what their father is currently doing for himself."

Poverty is one of the core drivers of poor health in urban neighborhoods.[39] African Americans and Hispanics who grow up in low-income urban neighborhoods are often exposed to factors such as neighborhood violence, food insecurity, and drug and alcohol abuse, and have higher rates of late-stage cancer and mental health issues such as anxiety and depression.[40] In the 1980s, the United States ranked in the top half when it came to our health indicators compared to our peer nations.[41] In the past 40 years, health overall has improved, but our rate of improvement has lagged substantially behind that of peer nations, bringing us down to the very bottom of the list in terms of health achievement.[42] Poverty is becoming more of an important risk factor for early death. Inequality is at an historic high, driving a gap between the wealthy and those experiencing poverty. It is at a level not seen since the Great Depression.[43]

Lack of Health Insurance and the Struggle to Afford Treatment

Many of us who live in urban neighborhoods have family members or friends who have passed away much earlier than expected from a heart attack, stroke, diabetes, HIV/AIDS, obesity, or gun violence. One factor in these deaths is the lack of health insurance. Over 30 million people still do not have coverage.[44] Even those who do have coverage still struggle to afford treatment, as insurance plans do not always cover the entire cost.[45] Josephine talked about how going to the doctor is no longer an option for her.

> Every time I have to go to the doctor, I have to call out from work, which means I don't get paid for the time I would have gotten had I worked my shift. I have to arrange for a babysitter and pay them by the hour, then take two city busses across town to see my doctor. Once there, in the doctor's office, I have to wait 30 minutes before a doctor can even see me. As if that is not enough, I still have my insurance to deal with. They help with some of my medications, but it's not enough. One of my medication bottles that only lasts a month cost me $400 every month. I don't have that type of money lying around. I can't afford that, not with what I bring home after they take taxes out of my check. I'm struggling just to get by—I'm literally living paycheck to paycheck. I simply can't do it. So I just don't take the medication.

The mother of my childhood friend, who I grew up with in Edenwald Houses, passed away from diabetes and living in poverty. Over the last 10 years of her life, she was rushed to the hospital's emergency room whenever she had complications from her diabetes. She did not have any insurance, and her family believed that was the reason she did not receive any quality care. Eventually she lost her foot and her mobility was restricted to a wheelchair, and ultimately she died from the disease.

Sabrina still gets frustrated about how poverty has taken the life of her younger sister. She stated,

I still get angry at the fact my younger sister died of liver disease. We know that her life could have been saved if she had gotten a liver transplant, but she was denied because she did not have health insurance. Three major hospitals turned her down. If it had not been for my strong faith in God and my church family, my sister's name would have been forgotten. People from my church held up signs with my sister's name on them outside the hospital, advocating for transplants and uninsured patients. We marched for days in front of all three hospitals, holding up signs, chanting my sister's name. On her death certificate, it states that she died of liver disease. That's a boldface lie. We know that the real cause of death was inequality and poverty. . . . The idea that poverty killed my sister is something that I have to live with for the rest of my life.

My grandmother's death was also a result of living in poverty. At the age of 70, she died of a stroke at Albert Einstein Hospital in the Bronx, New York. After she graduated from Grace H Dodge Career and Technical High School, she became a case manager for the New York City Department of Social Services for over 20 years. Even though she worked every single day and many of her friends who lived in the same public housing projects believed that she had a "good city job," because the workers' union protected her, she was still part of what many people would call the "poor working class."

A few years prior to her stroke, she needed heart surgery. During the procedure, they placed stents in her heart to prevent her from having a heart attack. Over the years, my grandmother put on an excessive amount of weight. She also had high blood pressure. As she began to age and moved into her early sixties, she had her first stroke. Then she had a second stroke. As a family we went to the hospital and sat by her side for hours. Eventually, her weight and high blood pressure became too much for her system to maintain.

The Rise of Childhood Poverty in Urban Neighborhoods

A complex issue related to poverty that at times is overlooked or never discussed is the rise of childhood poverty in urban neighborhoods. Josephine's son Sebastian noted,

> We never seem to ever have enough money to live a normal life like some of my friends in school. My mother is constantly getting eviction notices put on the door for unpaid rent. My real father always says he is going to take me and my sister school shopping for clothes, but never does. My mom has not bought me a pair of new sneakers in months and now I have holes in the bottom of my sneakers. My mother sometimes sends my sister and I over to her friend's house to have dinner with them from time to time so we will not have to go to bed hungry. . . . All of this because we are poor and live like bums.

In Cincinnati, Ohio, where Calvin and Sabrina have resided for 10 years, nearly 43% of children live below the federal poverty level.[46] That amounts to one in four children, or 45,845 children, living in poor urban neighborhoods.[47] People who live in poor urban neighborhoods and have lower incomes have shorter lives and are more often ill compared to those who live in higher-income urban neighborhoods.[48] Cincinnati children who come from high-income neighborhoods are expected to live up to 20 years longer than children who come from low-income neighborhoods.[49] Children who live in excess poverty are less likely to have access to preventative services and medications for conditions such as asthma.[50] This disparity can be seen even in neighborhoods right next to each other. Children in the 1970s and 1980s were healthier than today's adults.[51]

If we can't rely on the Equal Protection Clause of the Fourteenth Amendment and the courts to protect those living in poverty and recognize people experiencing poverty as a "suspect class," then we must ask if newly elected governmental officials in Congress can do anything about the current situation.

Notes

1. Rivera, "Puerto Rico's History."
2. Bradley, "The Curse of La Llorona."
3. Baker DeGuzman et al., "Impact of Urban Neighborhood Disadvantage."
4. Weber Buchholz, Huffman, and McKenna, "Overweight and Obese Low-Income Women."
5. Baker DeGuzman et al., "Impact of Urban Neighborhood Disadvantage."
6. Baker DeGuzman et al., "Impact of Urban Neighborhood Disadvantage."
7. Regelski, "The Soul of Food."
8. New York City Department of Health and Mental Hygiene, "Hypertension Hospitalizations."
9. New York City Department of Health and Mental Hygiene, "Hypertension Hospitalizations."
10. Dr. Joycelyn Elders was the first African American and the second woman to serve as the US surgeon general during the presidency of Bill Clinton in 1993. During her 15 months in office, amid skepticism from conservatives, Dr. Elders continued to discuss health issues that mattered, such as sex education and substance abuse.
11. Jehl, "Surgeon General Forced to Resign."
12. Galea and Vaughan, "Public Health of Consequence."
13. Galea and Vaughan, "Public Health of Consequence."
14. Danford et al., "Perceptions of Low-Income Mothers."
15. The National Survey of Children's Health was redesigned by the Maternal and Child Health Bureau in 2016 to provide rich data on children's lives, covering topics such as physical and mental health, access to health care, and neighborhoods.
16. Galea and Vaughan, "Public Health of Consequence."
17. Weber Buchholz, Huffman, and McKenna, "Overweight and Obese Low-Income Women."
18. Sanyaolu et al., "Childhood and Adolescent Obesity."
19. Hamzelou, "Wealth Can't Always Buy Health."
20. Hamzelou, "Wealth Can't Always Buy Health."
21. Wallace, "Health Disparities."
22. The Equal Protection Clause was intended to stop states from discriminating against Black people. The clause took effect in 1868, stating, "No State shall make or enforce any law which shall abridge the privileges or immunities of citizens of the United States; nor shall any State deprive any person of life, liberty, or property, without due process of law; nor deny to any person within its jurisdiction the equal protection of the laws." It mandates that people who have similar situations be treated equally.
23. Adrienne Rich was a feminist and one of the most widely read and influential poets of the second half of the twentieth century, and was known for

bringing the oppression of women to the forefront of politics in her poetry writings.

24. Galarneau, "Getting King's Words Right."
25. Galarneau, "Getting King's Words Right."
26. King, "Health Care Injustice."
27. King, "Beyond Vietnam."
28. Nice, "No Scrutiny Whatsoever."
29. Rose, "Poor as a Suspect Class."
30. Ross and Li, "Measuring Political Power."
31. Harris v. McRae, 448 U.S. 297 (1980), Justia US Supreme Court, https://supreme.justia.com/cases/federal/us/448/297/.
32. Maher v. Roe, 434 U.S. 647 (1977), US Supreme Court, https://scholar.google.com/scholar_case?case=10803349459097846233&q=maher+v.+roe&hl=en&as_sdt=6,36&as_vis=1.
33. Powell, "U.S. Reports: Maher v. Roe."
34. San Antonio v. Rodriguez, 411 U.S. 1 (1973), US Supreme Court, https://www.law.cornell.edu/supremecourt/text/411/1.
35. San Antonio v. Rodriguez, 411 U.S. 1 (1973), US Supreme Court, https://www.law.cornell.edu/supremecourt/text/411/1.
36. Noll, "San Antonio Independent School District v. Rodriguez."
37. Rose, "Poor as a Suspect Class."
38. Rose, "Poor as a Suspect Class."
39. Galea and Vaughan, "Public Health of Consequence."
40. Baker DeGuzman et al., "Impact of Urban Neighborhood Disadvantage."
41. Galea and Vaughan, "Public Health of Consequence."
42. Galea and Vaughan, "Public Health of Consequence."
43. Curnutte and DeMio, "More Suburban Cincinnati School Children."
44. Belluz, "What We Know."
45. Zucchi, "What Does Health Insurance Not Cover?"
46. Curnutte and DeMio, "More Suburban Cincinnati School Children."
47. Curnutte and DeMio, "More Suburban Cincinnati School Children."
48. Health Department, "Community Health Assessment."
49. Health Department, "Community Health Assessment."
50. Curnutte and DeMio, "More Suburban Cincinnati School Children."
51. Coughlan, "Childhood in the US."

Bibliography

Baker DeGuzman, Pam, Wendy F. Cohn, Fabian Camacho, Brandy L. Edwards, Vanessa N. Sturz, and Anneke T. Schroen. "Impact of Urban Neighborhood Disadvantage on Late Stage Breast Cancer Diagnosis in Virginia." *Journal of Urban Health* 94, no. 2 (2017): 199–210. https://doi.org/10.1007/s11524-017-0142-5.

Belluz, Julia. "What We Know about the 30 Million Americans Who Are Still Uninsured." *Vox*. Last updated April 7, 2017. https://www.vox.com/2017/4/7/15225800/30-million-americans-are-still-uninsured-inequality.

Bradley, Lora. "The Curse of La Llorona: The Real Legend Behind the Horror Film." *Vanity Fair*. Updated April 19, 2019. https://www.vanityfair.com/hollywood/2019/04/la-llorona-real-mexican-legend-curse-of-la-llorona-movie.

Coughlan, Sean. "Childhood in the US 'safer than in the 1970s.'" *BBC News*. Updated December 23, 2014. https://www.bbc.com/news/education-30578830.

Curnutte, Mark, and Terry DeMio. "More Suburban Cincinnati School Children in Poverty than Before the Great Recession." *Cincinnati Enquirer*. December 6, 2018. https://www.cincinnati.com/story/news/2018/12/06/more-suburban-cincinnati-school-kids-living-poverty-census-estimates-show/2152364002/.

Danford, Cynthia A., Celeste M. Schultz, Katherine Rosenblum, Allison L. Miller, and Julie C. Lumeng. "Perceptions of Low-Income Mothers about the Causes and Ways to Prevent Overweight in Children." *Child: Care, Health and Development* 41, no. 6 (2015): 865–72. https://dx.doi.org/10.1111%2Fcch.12256.

Forrest-Bank, Shandra S., Nicole Nicotera, Dawn Matera Bassett, and Peter Ferrarone. "Effects of an Expressive Art Intervention with Urban Youth in Low-Income Neighborhoods." *Child and Adolescent Social Work Journal* 33, no. 5 (2016): 429–41. https://doi.org/10.1007/s10560-016-0439-3.

Galarneau, Charlene. "Getting King's Words Right." *Journal of Health Care for the Poor and Underserved* 29 (2018): 5–8. https://muse.jhu.edu/article/686948/pdf.

Galea, Sandro, and Roger Vaughan. "A Public Health of Consequence: Review of the January 2017 Issue of AJPH." *American Journal of Public Health* 107, no. 1 (2017): 17–18. https://doi.org/10.2105/AJPH.2016.303540.

Goldberg, Mark. *Lessons from Exceptional School Leaders*. California: Association for Supervision and Curriculum Development, 2001.

Hamzelou, Jessica. "Wealth Can't Always Buy Health." *New Scientist*, April 2017.

Health Department. "Community Health Assessment." City of Cincinnati. Last updated December 21, 2017. https://www.cincinnati-oh.gov/sites/health/assets/File/EDIT%20THIS%20CHA_12_21_17%20FINAL(1).pdf.

Jehl, Douglas. "Surgeon General Forced to Resign by White House" *New York Times*. Updated December 10, 1994. https://www.nytimes.com/1994/12/10/us/surgeon-general-forced-to-resign-by-white-house.html.

King, Martin Luther, Jr. "Beyond Vietnam—A Time to Break Silence." American Rhetoric Online Speech Bank. Last updated January 3, 2021. https://www.americanrhetoric.com/speeches/mlkatimetobreaksilence.htm.

King, Martin Luther, Jr. "Dr. Martin Luther King on Health Care Injustice." https://pnhp.org/news/dr-martin-luther-king-on-health-care-injustice/.

Mansyur, Carol L., Valory N. Pavlik, David J. Hyman, Wendell C. Taylor, and G. Kenneth Goodrick. "Self-Efficacy and Barriers to Multiple Behavior Change in Low-Income African Americans with Hypertension." *Journal of Behavioral Medicine* 36, no. 1 (2013): 75–85. https://doi.org/10.1007/s10865-012-9403-7.

May, Lucy. "New Census Data Show Greater Cincinnati's Child Poverty Rate Improved, but Lots of Work Remains." *WCPO 9 News* (Cincinnati, OH). Last updated December 11, 2018. https://www.wcpo.com/news/local-news/hamilton-county/cincinnati/new-census-data-show-greater-cincinnati-s-child-poverty-rate-improved-but-lots-of-work-remains.

Ness, Maria, Danielle T. Barradas, Jennifer Irving, and Susan E. Manning. "Correlates of Overweight and Obesity among American Indian/Alaska Native and Non-Hispanic White Children and Adolescents: National Survey of Children's Health, 2007." *Maternal and Child Health Journal* 16, suppl. 2 (2012): 268–77. https://doi.org/10.1007/s10995-012-1191-8.

New York City Department of Health and Mental Hygiene. "Hypertension Hospitalizations and Related Morbidity in New York City." *Epi Data Brief* 1, no. 83 (2016): 1–8. https://www1.nyc.gov/assets/doh/downloads/pdf/epi/databrief83.pdf.

Nice, Julie A. "No Scrutiny Whatsoever: Deconstitutionalization of Poverty Law, Dual Rules of Law, and Dialogic Default." *Fordham Urban Law Journal* 35, no. 3 (2008): 629–71. https://ir.lawnet.fordham.edu/ulj/vol35/iss3/4.

Nohlen, D. "2000 Puerto Rican General Elections." Wikiwand. Updated December 10, 2005. https://www.wikiwand.com/en/2000_Puerto_Rican_general_election.

Noll, Carl F. "San Antonio Independent School District v. Rodriguez: A Retreat from Equal Protection." *Cleveland State Law Review* 22, no. 3 (1973): 585–601.

Ogden, Cynthia L., Susan Z. Yanovski, Margaret D. Carroll, and Katherine M. Flegal. "The Epidemiology Of Obesity." *Gastroenterology* 132, no. 6 (2007): 2087–102. https://doi.org/10.1053/j.gastro.2007.03.052.

Powell, Lewis F., Jr. "U.S. Reports: Maher v. Roe, 432 U.S. 464 (1977)." *US Reports* 432, no 36 (1976). https://www.loc.gov/item/usrep432464/.

Regelski, Christina. "The Soul of Food: Slavery's Influence on Southern Cuisine." Accessed November 19, 2020. https://ushistoryscene.com/article/slavery-southern-cuisine/.

Rivera, Magaly. "Puerto Rico's History: 1950–2022." Accessed December 10, 2018. https://welcome.topuertorico.org/history6.shtml.

Rose, Henry. "The Poor as a Suspect Class under the Equal Protection Clause: An Open Constitutional Question." *Nova Law Review* 34, no. 407 (2010): 408–19. https://dx.doi.org/10.2139/ssrn.1546666.

Ross, Bertrall L., II, and Su Li. "Measuring Political Power: Suspect Class Determinations and the Poor." *California Law Review* 104, no. 2 (2016): 323–90.

Sanyaolu, Adekunle, Chuka Okorie, Xiaohua Qi, Jennifer Locke, and Saif Rehman. "Childhood and Adolescent Obesity in the United States: A Public Health Concern." *Global Pediatric Health* 6 (2019). https://doi.org/10.1177%2F2333794X19891305.

Wallace, Edward V. "Health Disparities: Using Policies to Rethink Our Strategies for Eliminating the Impact of Food Deserts by Focusing on Unhealthy Dietary Patterns." *Journal of Public Affairs* 19, no. 3 (2018): 1–7. https://doi.org/10.1002/pa.1875.

Weber Buchholz, Susan, Dolores Huffman, and Joy Christine McKenna. "Overweight and Obese Low-Income Women: Restorative Health Behaviors Under Overwhelming Conditions." *Health Care for Women International* 33, no. 2 (2012): 182–97. https://doi.org/10.1080/07399332.2011.630115.

Weigel, M. Margaret, Rodrigo X. Armijos, Marcia Racines, and William Cevallos. "Food Insecurity Is Associated with Undernutrition but Not Overnutrition in Ecuadorian Women from Low-Income Urban Neighborhoods." *Journal of Environmental and Public Health* 2016 (2016): 8149459. https://doi.org/10.1155/2016/8149459.

Zucchi, Kristina. "What Does Health Insurance Not Cover? Find Out Which Services Most Plans Decline." Investopedia. Updated March 27, 2022. https://www.investopedia.com/articles/insurance/09/services-health-insurers-do-not-cover.asp.

FIVE

Health Disparities in Urban Neighborhoods

I F A NURSE or a doctor from the 1970s could time-travel to today's health care system, they would not recognize much, if any, of it.[1] Back in the 1970s, patients and their families had to follow hierarchies and strict rules. Only two immediate family members were allowed to visit a loved one in the hospital. Children under the age of 14 were not allowed to see a family member during visiting hours. Doctors did not share your health information with other physicians, and getting results from lab work took days.

Today, doctors can use their electronic tablets to see notes put in your chart by other physicians. People have immediate access to their lab results, and all of this can be checked from their cell phones, tablets, or personal computers.[2] We can communicate with our primary physician, cardiologist, gynecologist, and oncologist at almost any time and from anywhere. But this shift in communication and technological advancement has also helped create health inequalities in low-income urban neighborhoods.

In the 1960s and 1970s, paper records were used to share health information. I can remember going to a shoebox under my grandmother's bed to find her medical statements. Even then, I knew there had to be a better way. Today, if my grandmother were still alive, I could use my laptop to help her log onto MyChart, and she could have access to all of her health information.

The rapid changes that have occurred due to technological advancement over the last few decades have had significant effects on the lives of many people. However, this is not true of every low-income urban neighborhood. When I worked and lived in Birmingham, Alabama, the Worley family did not own a personal computer or laptop. If they wanted to obtain health information, they had to go to the local library, which was approximately 20 minutes away by car. When I visited the home of Richard and Cynthia Coleman, they owned a few electronics, such as a 50-inch television and a CD player. They did not own a computer, nor did they have access to health information. Lack of access to information is not a new phenomenon, especially regarding health care.

The "Damaging Constitution"

I often refer to the Constitution—the document responsible for establishing federal laws and fundamental rights—as the "Damaging Constitution." The "Damaging Constitution" explains in clear language that certain rights (food inspections, health care services, providing accurate consumer health information) do not exist as a constitutional issue, requiring the federal government to take action; rather these are matters to be taken up at the local or state level.[3]

Local and state governments have the power to regulate standards of behavior and maintain order to protect the safety and well-being of the public. All too often, this power is exercised in ways that work against those goals. For example, New York City's "stop-and-frisk" policy allowed police officers to stop and frisk individuals on the sole base of "reasonable suspicion." After years of this abusive practice, a federal judge ruled that New York City Police Department stop-and-frisk tactics violated the Fourth Amendment and was only used as a method of racially profiling and harassing Black and Latino citizens.[4] Such uses of "police power" are intended to be intimidating and hostile.

If we assess police power, we see that the way the Constitution is interpreted by the US Supreme Court means that the court can only make a recommendation—not a mandate—to the states to act in the best interest of the public. The Constitution does not require local and state governments to provide any goods or services to the public whatsoever. The people who wrote the Constitution were not concerned that the government would do too little for the people, but that it might do too much.[5] But in attempting to protect citizens from governmental overreach, the Constitution actually leaves many people unprotected. This is why I call it the "Damaging Constitution."

For example, a number of district court judges have shut down the idea that individuals are required to have health insurance under the Affordable Care Act. The courts ruled that this mandate was unconstitutional.[6] A number of appeals were filed against the district courts, and in June 2021, the Supreme Court dismissed a lawsuit against the Affordable Care Act, allowing millions of people to keep their insurance coverage during the COVID-19 pandemic.

Not requiring the government to provide goods and services to the public—such as health care, health information, and technology—perpetuates a cycle of health inequities. For example, technology, a tool that is supposed to level the playing field, has actually un-leveled the playing field. A study by a group of researchers came to a surprising and distressing conclusion: in many cases, technology is not the great equalizer of health and education. In actuality, technology has the opposite effect.[7]

Digital Divide: Blacks and Whites Use Technology Differently

The "digital divide" refers to a lack of access to technology for people living in poverty in low-income neighborhoods. But this is just part of the problem. Rich kids from affluent backgrounds and kids from low-income families and urban neighborhoods use technology differently. White children select different programs and apps and engage in different mental activities compared to Black children and come away with different kinds of knowledge, which creates different experiences and, ultimately, ongoing disparities.[8] When talking with Shelia Blackmon, she explained to me how she sees the difference in how kids of different races and ethnicities use technology.

> Every time my grandson D-Jay comes to visit Lester and I, he locks himself in the bedroom for hours and is playing video games. One time he had his headset on and was playing video games with his friend "Little Man." Don't ask me why they call him that, but everyone does. Anyway, he is a nice respectful Black child who always speaks. At least, he always speaks to me when I see him, and he lives in the apartment complex right next to ours [*pointing her finger*]. Other times I've seen him invite other people over [white friends], but they are not just playing video games, they are also talking about creating video games. To me, that is the difference between them and us. My grandson and his friend who lives in the apartment complex next to me, all they want to do is play the video games all day, but white kids . . . they want to design the video games. I'm constantly telling him I don't just want him to have a piece of the American pie, I want him to have the ingredients.

Mass Media and the Stigmatization of People in Poverty

Early television in the United States was quite primitive. Before 1947, the number of people who owned a television in their home could be measured in the thousands.[9] In addition, there were only three major broadcasting networks: ABC, NBC, and CBS.[10] In the 1970s, television sets only had 12 free channels and the broadcasting station would automatically be turned off by one or two o'clock in the morning. By the late 1990s, television had changed drastically—98% of US homes had at least one television set,[11] and TV was used in many ways as a tool to bring people together. Now, with the increasing availability of cable subscription services, satellite TV, and livestreaming, television is becoming more and more fragmented.[12] Unlike before, when television programs were made to attract a wider audience, TV news shows today are designed to attract smaller audiences of a definite age group, income level, racial makeup, and political affiliation, such as Fox News, MSNBC, and CNN.[13]

Many accuse mass media of being directly responsible for urban health disparities—that it portrays people of color as impoverished recipients of welfare, absentee fathers, violent, lazy, and criminals.[14] Historically, the media has not always stigmatized poverty and welfare, nor made it a Black and brown issue. In the 1920s and 1930s, white men benefited from anti-poverty programs such as welfare. When white men were unemployed and struggling to enter the workforce, the media did not classify them as lazy or hopeless individuals. They were typically thought of as having run into hard luck or just needing some government support to help them get through the tough times.[15]

But the media has worked endlessly to pathologize poor Blacks in the American imagination to justify slavery, mass incarceration, widespread economic inequality, and urban disparities. One study reviewed more than 800 local and national news stories and published commentaries between January 2015 and December 2016, randomly sampling some of the most highly rated news programs for each of the major broadcast and cable networks, such as ABC, CBS, Fox News, CNN, and MSNBC.[16] The study also consisted of newspapers such as the *New York Post*, *Washington Post*, *Wall Street Journal*, *New York Times*, *USA Today*, *Los Angeles Times*, and *Chicago Tribune*. The study concluded that both news sources (newspapers and broadcast networks) shaped false narratives about Blacks to the public, stating that they were "pathological and undeserving."[17]

The study also found that Black people represent 59% of those living in poverty that are portrayed by the media, but only account for 29% of Americans living in poverty. On the other hand, whites represent 17% of those experiencing poverty, as described in the news media, but consist of 66% of Americans living in poverty in our society.[18] Furthermore, Black people represent 37% percent of the criminals presented in the news, but consist of only 26% of those who are arrested on criminal charges. Yet white people are portrayed as criminals in the news media just 28% of the time, when FBI crime reports show they make up 77% of the crime suspects in America.[19] It is my belief, along with other health disparity scholars, that when the news media puts out warped portrayals and writes outlandish narratives about people from vulnerable populations who live in urban areas, there are real and dire consequences that impact the life and health of people from underserved neighborhoods, such as racial profiling by the police, harsher sentences from judges, less attention from doctors, and negative health policies by political leaders. In a study, researchers examined the framing of individuals using an article that contained misinformation. The sole purpose of the article and its misinformation was to evoke a negative portrayal of former President Barack Obama. The misinformation was purposely designed to make former President Obama look as if he was struggling to maintain popularity by appearing on television shows. The results showed that participants that viewed negative stereotypes in the article were more likely to present racist beliefs.[20]

The Shutting Down of Urban Hospitals

Increasing numbers of at-risk hospitals are shutting down and changing the health landscape of low-income neighborhoods. As a result, families such as the Hugheses, Worleys, Ruizes, and Colemans have fewer options when it comes to receiving hospital care due to emergency department closures. These closures have negative health repercussions for the community.[21]

The declining of hospitals over the years in the United States has been gradual in low-income urban neighborhoods.[22] Before we had hospitals, health care was mainly provided by charities and primarily treated those experiencing poverty.[23] However, between 1900 and 1948, the emerging middle class began to struggle to access treatment and health care, which led them to be willing to pay general practitioners a fee for service.[24] This allowed the middle class and the wealthy to influence hospitals in deciding who could receive treatment and where they could receive it.

In New York City, hospitals are becoming non-existent. Since 2003, 15 hospitals have shut down. The most recent was St. Vincent's Hospital Manhattan, an urban hospital known for its charity care, which had to close its doors because the 160-year-old hospital was more than

$1 billion in debt.[25] A federal bill signed by former President Bill Clinton led hospitals that served the impoverished and elderly, such as St. Vincent's, into bankruptcy because of medical inflation and the lack of Medicaid and Medicare reimbursements.[26] For families and individuals who live in low-income urban neighborhoods, the closing of hospitals is about more than just the physical proximity. The problem also involves other barriers that families like the Ruizes might have to endure in a new hospital setting, such as language barriers and high deductibles and co-pays, which contribute to health disparities and adversely affect everyone living in low-income urban neighborhoods.

During the COVID-19 pandemic of 2020–2022, many New York City hospitals, predominately those in Black and Hispanic communities, were hit hard.[27] Even before the pandemic, many hospitals in New York City were understaffed, underresourced, and lacked medical equipment. During the pandemic, these facilities faced widespread shortages of masks, ventilators, testing equipment, and other protective gear.

In Delaware, where the Coleman family resides, the closures of hospitals have impacted those living in poverty and those without insurance in many ways. The Delaware Department of Health and Social Services shut down the Emily P. Bissell Hospital permanently in 2015 due to ongoing problems with the hospital.[28] Richard Coleman told me about how, within a matter of years, hospitals have gotten worse.

> We have it bad, real bad. I remember when there were tons of doctors at the hospital, maybe about 40 or so doctors, then the next thing I know, in a matter of months, right before the hospital shut down, there was only about 12 doctors working at the hospital. Tell me, how do you take care of an entire community of people that is sick with only 12 doctors? I would not want to go to the hospital to be treated for a gunshot wound, only to find out I may not be seen right away because there are only 12 doctors at the hospital. This is horrifying, and it's poor people like myself who have to live with it every day. But this is what happens when you put profit over the patient's health.

There are a number of reasons for the closing of hospitals in urban neighborhoods in Delaware. As the cost of living continues to rise, so does the cost of medical care.[29] Many hospitals in urban neighborhoods that serve those living in poverty are financially challenged.[30] They are closing because of money-losing decisions made internally or externally beyond their control. Unexpected expenses, such as plumbing problems, flooding that renders the facility unusable, and not having hot water has played a role in the shutdown of hospitals in urban neighborhoods.[31] With extensive repairs to hospitals comes the disruption of operations and services needed for hospitals to function.

Sometimes a hospital closes because it is considered to be the weakest link in the network of hospitals that serves the public.[32] For example, a CEO of a major urban hospital announced that it would be closing, along with all its clinics, because of the financial strain it was putting on the entire system and how it was compromising other hospitals in the network. In the three years of ownership under the CEO, the system absorbed more than $17 million dollars in operating losses.[33] In many instances, when a hospital cannot offer certain services to the communities it is supposed to serve, compared to another for-profit hospital in a competitive market, the former hospital will be forced to merge with another institution or close.

In Alabama, large teaching hospitals such as the University of Alabama at Birmingham Hospital have been entering into alliances with smaller hospitals in urban neighborhoods to prevent them from shutting down. Recently, the University of Alabama at Birmingham Health System merged with Ascension St. Vincent's Birmingham Health System.[34] On the surface, the collaboration between these two hospitals seems to be a good strategy to address health disparities in low-income urban neighborhoods and provide access to services for vulnerable populations. However, this could not be further from the truth—especially for the Worley family. For the Worleys, this merger means more crowding at the hospital because now there is only one facility as opposed to two. It means that the Worleys might experience longer wait times when seeing a doctor and possibly even leave the hospital without being seen, forgoing medical treatment altogether, because they had to travel such a long distance to the hospital, when before all they had to do was walk a few blocks to get treatment. Frank Worley spoke about how he was tricked into thinking that the hospital merger was a great idea. He stated,

> On the outside, these two hospitals coming together gave me the impression that the merger was something that would help out poor people in the local neighborhood. I mean, the lawn was cut, the sprinkling system was on, and the lights were lit up at night, making everything look pretty, but when you got on the inside it was a zoo. I mean, people were everywhere, it was just too overcrowded.

For a high-income neighborhood, the merging or shutting down of a hospital is not as much of a problem. For instance, many people who live in high-income neighborhoods own cars and have money they can use to take other forms of transportation, such as Uber or Lyft, to a hospital to receive treatment if they need to see a physician. However, this may not be the case for families living in low-income urban neighborhoods; for them, no longer being able to walk a few blocks to be seen by a doctor at a local hospital in one's neighborhood results in major health consequences.[35] There are a few evidence-based studies on this topic. One study, perhaps unsurprisingly, suggests that increased distances to the nearest hospital resulted in larger barriers to care for patients and a greater decline in health status[36]—as an example, putting pregnant women and their babies at risk by having to travel for delivery. More public health policies need to be enacted to make sure that if a hospital merges with another institution or shuts down in a low-income urban neighborhood, the impact will be minimal and the quality of health care will be guaranteed for vulnerable populations living in low-income urban neighborhoods. We need to ensure that when decisions are being made about hospital closures, equity is being taken into consideration despite the size of the hospital and its financial hardship.

The District of Greenwood: "Black Wall Street"

Across the country, there has been a major demographic shift in urban neighborhoods, with a rising number of successful Blacks and Latinos moving out of urban neighborhoods to live in rural and suburban communities.[37] During the 1900s, one of the benefits of living in a segregated community was that Blacks could count on one another during the good times and the bad.[38] In Tulsa, Oklahoma, the district of Greenwood was one of the most affluent African American communities in the United States for the early part of the twentieth century. What was so special about Greenwood was that it was self-contained and self-sufficient, and—most importantly—Black-owned.[39] You had your banks, grocery stores, libraries, hotels, barbershops, hair salons, luxury stores, and offices for doctors, lawyers, and dentists. Not to mention luxuries, such as indoor plumbing and a remarkable school system that educated highly intelligent Black children. Greenwood even had a bus and taxi service, a post office, a hospital, and more, all lined up in one neighborhood.[40] It was also home to many African Americans experiencing poverty. A significant number of people worked as janitors, dishwashers, maids, and porters. It was possible that if you were destitute and wanted to own a business, Greenwood had a system in place where you could get a loan and not be discriminated against.[41] What made Greenwood the epicenter for African Americans was the socially conscious mindset of the people who lived and worked in the district. They understood that in order for Greenwood to be successful and sustain a healthy quality of life, every dollar within the district needed to change hands 19 times before it could leave the community. Greenwood was so progressive during its time that it was given the name "Black Wall Street." It was a community built for Black people, by Black people.

After years of prosperity and fortune in Tulsa's unapologetic Black community, jealous less-fortunate whites had a desire to put high-achieving African Americans in their place by sparking two days of racial violence. We began to see the deterioration of neighborhoods such as Greenwood—mainly because many whites resented the upscale lifestyle of Blacks, who they viewed as inferior.[42] The Ku Klux Klan savagely and brutally perpetuated violence against Tulsa's sophisticated Black citizens, where businesses were burned, Blacks were lynched and shot in the head, homes were looted, and cultural and public institutions were destroyed.[43]

Spatial Mismatch: Impact on Access to Employment

Today, we can look at spatial mismatch and spatial racism as contributing factors to the fall of urban neighborhoods. Spatial mismatch occurs when Blacks and Latinos who live in urban neighborhoods do not have access to jobs because these jobs are located in suburban areas, difficult if not impossible to reach by public transportation.[44] From the 1930s to the 2000s, we have seen job growth relocating to the suburbs where many whites tend to live and Blacks remaining concentrated in urban areas, where they appear to be increasingly living in worse conditions than those in the suburbs.[45] This might explain the decline in Black male employment, making it difficult for Black males to provide for their family and community, which ultimately contributes to fallen urban neighborhoods because of job suburbanization.

Effects of Spatial Racism

Spatial racism continues to have a profound effect on wealth and opportunity. In the late 1970s and 1980s, when college-educated African Americans began to leave their neighborhoods in the inner city and voluntarily move to the suburbs to invest in homeownership, their levels of education, businesses, social networks, and other resources also left these neighborhoods. As more and more African Americans continue this pattern of fleeing urban neighborhoods and isolating themselves from Black people living in poverty, the cycle of poverty will repeat itself, allowing the wealth, education, and health gap to grow even larger.[46]

Let me be clear: I am not against anyone wanting to better themselves by furthering their education. The problem with spatial racism is that once people of color have acquired the "American Dream," oftentimes they do not go back to their former neighborhoods and uplift the next generation. When I asked Samantha Hughes what she saw herself doing for a career, her immediate response was, "I want to be a pediatric nurse." When asked if she happened to know an African American pediatric nurse and whether a pediatric nurse lived in her neighborhood, she told me, "I have never met a Black pediatric nurse before and never seen one in the neighborhood since I've been living here . . . and I was born and raised in this neighborhood." Research has shown that when Black children don't see Black doctors, Black lawyers, Black teachers, and other Black professionals, it is difficult for them to see themselves in these occupations because they don't see and interact with these Black role models on a day-to-day basis.[47]

We see spatial racism existing in other arenas as well, such as education. Some of the first Historically Black Colleges and Universities (HBCUs), which include Hampton University, Fisk University, Spelman College, and Morehouse College, were mainly created for the Black upper class or elite and the Black middle class. Students who attended these colleges and universities attended these schools to develop skills, learn their history and culture, and obtain knowledge that put them in a separate class to become engineers, lawyers, doctors, politicians, accountants, teachers, and business executives. These students were expected, as a social responsibility, to go give back to their communities and train the next generation of young scholars.

For years, Spelman College, Howard University, Hampton University, and Morehouse College were considered to be premier institutions and listed in the top 25 national rankings amongst all Historically Black Colleges and Universities.[48] For instance, Spelman College was the only HBCU ranked by the *U.S. News & World Report* among its top 100 liberal arts colleges. Howard University, often considered to be the "Black Harvard," was the first HBCU featured in the publication of National University Rankings.[49]

These days, one of the hallmarks of spatial racism is many of our best and brightest young Black students not attending HBCUs as in years past. Fifty years ago, at least 90% of Black students attended HBCUs, because they were more likely to succeed than if they attended

Predominantly White Institutions (PWIs). Currently, that number has dropped to 9%.[50] In fact, due to the decline in student enrollment, many HBCUs are on the verge of closing. For example, Bennett University, South Carolina State University, and Wilberforce University are millions of dollars in debt and in danger of shutting down.[51] Because of spatial racism, it is not a matter of if these HBCUs will close, but when. Furthermore, it's safe to say that when these schools close, more than likely these institutions will not be replaced and the students will be the ones to suffer from the loss of them.[52] Not only will their education be taken away, but also the heritage and traditions that come along with attending a Historically Black College and University.

Today, many of our most talented and gifted Black students receive full academic and athletic scholarships to attend top-tier schools such as Harvard, Yale, Duke University, the University of Alabama, Princeton University, University of North Carolina at Chapel Hill, University of Kentucky, and Cornell University. All these institutions, at one point or another, were not interested in accepting African American students into their academic programs. Students from the Black upper and middle class were not being sought out by these prestigious institutions during the 1920s and 1930s, but now are being cherry-picked so that many of these schools of higher learning can make the claim in their mission statements that they support "diversity, equity, and inclusion."[53] If we are being completely honest, many Predominantly White Institutions say they value diversity, but Black students don't get the proper support to be successful at Predominantly White Institutions and oftentimes have to deal with issues of racism. According to national news reports, "Predominantly White Institutions heavily recruit Black students, but they don't make it a welcoming environment."[54]

Trauma: From Incarceration to Victims of Violence

Everyday trauma in low-income urban neighborhoods is one of the key components in the surge of health disparities. Trauma is one of the most under-addressed mental health issues for people who live in low-income neighborhoods. Trauma can impact anyone, but tends to be heightened when people are living in poverty.[55] Traumatic events come in all forms, such as the loss of life or a threat to one's life, the loss of freedom or a threat to one's freedom, abuse (physical, sexual, emotional, even financial), and neglect. Some researchers think that having a distressing or disturbing experience or witnessing a traumatic event can have a devastating impact on an individual's mental and physical health, particularly when they live in neighborhoods where there are high concentrations of poverty.[56]

Do these traumatic events lead to chronic stress and health disparities for people who live in low-income neighborhoods? Does childhood trauma affect a person's adulthood, and is it associated with diminishing health outcomes for people who live in low-income neighborhoods? Is it impossible to achieve physical health if emotional needs are not met? Do these traumatic events truly change or influence health policies for people who live in low-income neighborhoods? The answer depends on which low-income neighborhood you study and how you examine the data.

In Birmingham, where Frank and Felicia Worley and their three children, Darryl, Jamal, and Chris, live, there is a great amount of concern when it comes to parental incarceration because it disproportionately affects lower-income households, mainly Black families. Felicia states,

My husband and I are deeply concerned—we have seen the television documentaries about prison where they say children of incarcerated parents are six times more likely to be incarcerated as adults, especially if they live in neighborhoods where there is a great deal of poverty. Let's face it, we are poor and I have three Black boys. So yes, I'm scared to death that if my husband or I get hauled off to prison, that my boys are not far behind. How does that saying go again . . . the apple does not fall far from the tree.

A study found that Black men and women with no history of conviction or imprisonment earned less than white men and women with a criminal record. The same study concluded that by the end of a career, white men and women with a criminal record earned about $49,000 a year compared to Black men and women with no criminal records, who earned $39,000 over the same time period.[57]

Research among young children in Alabama who parents have been incarcerated has shown higher rates of depression and aggression.[58] One study found that African American children whose mother and father have both been incarcerated displayed higher levels of depression compared to children who have only one or none of their parents incarcerated.[59] Another study found that boys whose fathers were incarcerated in the state of Alabama were five times more likely to show levels of aggression compared to boys whose fathers never went to jail or prison.[60]

Unfortunately, parental incarceration is just one stressful, traumatic event that can impact the health of individuals living in low-income neighborhoods. If we were to look at the entire process of the criminal system—arrests, pre-trial, detention, trial, taking a plea, conviction, probation, jail, imprisonment, and parole—we would see many opportunities for people to be affected, and ultimately their overall health diminishes.[61]

Most of the trauma that people experience in low-income urban neighborhoods falls under the umbrella of violence. Studies show that the majority of traumatic events come from directly experiencing violence or learning that violence has occurred to a close family member, friend, or someone of the same racial identity within the community.[62] Studies from the National Crime Victimization Survey show that urban African Americans are more likely than whites and suburban and rural African Americans to be victims of a violent crime.[63] The Hugheses' youngest son, Thomas, noted,

> I remember when Brandon and I took our bikes out for a ride in the projects, we were riding in the park and four guys came up to my brother and me and said they liked our brand-new sneakers. One of the guys put his foot right next to mine and stated we wore the same shoe size and wanted for me to take my sneakers off. . . . Before I knew it, I got sucker-punched in the face and I fell off my bike. The next thing I know, two guys were holding me down while my sneakers were being snatched off my feet. By the time my

brother Brandon jumped off his bike to try and help me, they were running down the street. Brandon told me to get on my bike and let's go before they circled the block and came back to take his brand-new sneakers. . . . I will never forget that day. . . . I mean, that day I got my sneakers taken away continues to haunt me to this day. Every time I think about how people treated me in my own neighborhood makes me want to hurt somebody. I'm getting angry just talking about it. . . . What makes me really angry is that my mother had just bought me those sneakers from Dr. Jay's on Fordham Road. Those four guys don't know what my mom had to do to buy me those sneakers and they don't even care. That's what I have a problem with.

This is a major problem for the Hughes family. Brandon and Thomas know that violence in their neighborhood happens daily. They both have been victims of violence at one point or another in their neighborhood over the years, and they are well aware of the psychological impact this has had on them.

Urban studies experts who have tried to understand the impact of experiencing violence from the victim's perspective have found different results from other scholars. For example, homicide rates for Black males are 26.77 per 100,000 compared to 2.67 per 100,000 of their white counterparts, and they are approximately three times more likely than white men to be victims of a crime.[64] However, these scholars found that not all Black males who experience violence have lasting negative outcomes. Despite experiencing a traumatic event, such as being physically assaulted, many Black men do go on to become successful in their lives, such as becoming doctors, lawyers, accountants, and schoolteachers.[65] This is because trauma is not permanent and can be blocked out. After addressing their trauma directly, Black men often develop and maintain a positive outlook, as opposed to becoming vengeful and wanting to "clap back" at those who have caused them pain.

Similarly, learning that violence has occurred to a family member, close friend, or someone of the same racial identity as oneself is another traumatic event that can be related to health disparities and typically impacts the mental health of people living in urban neighborhoods. For example, the killings of unarmed Black and Latino men such as Eric Garner of New York City, Samuel DuBose of Cincinnati, Magdiel Sanchez of Oklahoma City, Oscar Ramirez Jr. of Los Angeles, Botham Jean of Dallas, and George Floyd of Minneapolis have been a mental trigger that has had a major impact on the mental health of people living in Black and Latino communities.[66] Josephine Rubio remembers when the police gunned down an innocent man in her neighborhood. She states,

> I remember when my best friend's brother was killed in these streets. He had two things working against him, he was Black and he was poor. They did not have to gun him down like that—all he was doing was selling fake leather purses on the sidewalk. . . . When the police approached him and told him he did not have a license to sell purses and that he needed to move from that location, they claim he got confrontational and reached for a weapon in his pocket. That's when they shot him multiple times. I will never forget the amount of blood that was in the street. Of course my friend's family never got justice, even when there were witnesses who saw everything, including myself. They treat us like we aren't worth anything.

Eloise Stevenson talked about her traumatic event from when she was a child. She stated,

> When I was younger, my sisters and I had to walk several miles to school every day. We did not have a car, so my mother told us that we had to walk and so we did. I remember one particular day, when I was cutting through the woods headed home, I saw a Black man hanging from a tree with his hands tied behind his back and a rope wrapped around his neck. All I could do at the moment was run home as fast as I could until I reached my front porch. I was terrified for days after I saw that. I know it was years ago, but I still have bad dreams from time to time.

It is not hard to understand how the lynching of Black men and women in this country has caused trauma in the Black community. Look at what they did to George Floyd—a cop put his knee on Floyd's neck. In Floyd's case, the police officer's knee was the rope—that was a lynching, just like the one Eloise Stevenson saw when she was a young girl. They are still killing us Black folks; they are just finding different ways to do it, and psychologically, it is causing us mental trauma and damage.

One of the reasons that the Ruiz family never had any children was that a few years back, Mercedes started to feel intense paranoia. Oftentimes she would ask her husband Ferdinand to call off from work, because she feared that he would come in contact with the police and not come back home from a hard day's work. Seeing unarmed Black and Latino men murdered in her neighborhood by the police was a physical and emotional trauma that she could not handle. Is it possible to achieve physical, emotional, spiritual, and social health if a person's mental health needs are not met? The answer is no. The five dimensions of health are interrelated; they are not separate from one another. There must be equilibrium: physical, emotional, spiritual, social, and mental health must all be in balance with one another to achieve wellness and build resistance against trauma.

Mercedes has also been terrified to bring a child into the world because of the experiences Latino men must endure in the United States. Her way of showing ultimate love is to not have any kids and take any risk of them being harmed in a world that does not value the lives of unarmed Black and Latino men. According to researchers, police killings of unarmed Black and Latino men contribute to 55 million additional poor mental health days every year among Black and Latino Americans in the United States.[67] That means that the mental trauma caused by police killings of unarmed Black and Latino men is nearly as great as the number of Black and Latinos who suffer from diabetes.[68] The death of a loved one that was shot by a police officer can be tragic for a family or community of any race; however, there is a deeper trauma present for Blacks and Latinos, whether or not they are related to the victim.

Suffering from Historical Trauma as Opposed to Post-traumatic Stress Disorder

Trauma has been part of history for people of color for centuries. Ultimately, when we talk about traumatic events that occur to a group of people, we are talking specifically about something known as historical trauma.[69] This is not to be confused with post-traumatic stress disorder (PTSD). When a person suffers from PTSD, a traumatic event affects just that individual. For instance, when a young Black man from a low-income neighborhood cuts through the park on his way home from school, and suddenly the police draw their guns and tell him to get on his knees or they will shoot because they suspect him to be a drug dealer, this individual will most likely find it difficult to survive encounters with law enforcement in the future. Every time this young man walks past a park or his friends mention that they want to go to the park and shoot hoops, this young man will relive the traumatic experience of being approached by police officers and being forced to his knees while a gun is pointed at his head. This is post-traumatic stress disorder. It is like a movie being played in the individual's brain over and over again without the person having the ability to turn it off.

However, historical trauma focuses on how traumatic events impact a group of people rather than the individual. Its focus is genocidal, as historical trauma has the ability to be passed on from one generation to the next.[70] For example, when we look at the system of enslavement for African Americans, we see that people of African descent were brutally whipped, made to pick cotton, forbidden to read or write, raped—only to watch their children be sold to white slave owners—and had their names changed, their identity stolen, and their culture destroyed. Despite the fact that our modern-day society is five to six generations removed from slavery, the trauma from slavery still manifests itself both personally and socially. When Black parents and grandparents tell their children and grandchildren, "You have to work twice as hard to get half as far, being a Black person in white America," what they are saying is that Black people never have been—and many of them never will be—accepted into the "American Dream." This is historical trauma. The parents and grandparents have internalized the views of the oppressor and are reinforcing the idea to their children and grandchildren that strength has to be measured by how much "pain" you can endure, physically, emotionally, and mentally.[71] This can manifest itself into self-hate and feelings of inferiority if the children and grandchildren internalize that they are not worthy or strong enough to get their hands on the "American Dream."

Historical trauma can also be found among Latino immigrants who leave their homelands and migrate to the United States in search of safety, shelter, and the "American Dream." Many Latinos experience trauma in the migration process in search of a better life for themselves and their families. The migration process has three points during which trauma can affect the psychological well-being of a group of people and negatively influence their health. First, when Latinos plan to flee their homeland, it is because they are faced with the trauma of extreme poverty, rape, abuse, war, and violence.[72] Oftentimes, these pre-migration traumas lead to hopelessness and depression. Second, trauma can occur to a group of people while the migration is happening in real time, especially for women. Women are often captured, sold into bondage, sexually assaulted, and forced into free labor.[73] Finally, after Latinos have survived the trauma in their homeland and the traumas along their journey, they still face trauma after arriving in the United States. Latinos enter the United States with hopes of finding a job, access to health care, and better education for their children, only to be welcomed with poor schools, unemployment, no health insurance, discrimination, poor housing conditions, and the constant threat of being deported back to their homeland, all of which lead to a cycle of trauma and negative health outcomes for the next generation and the generation after that to endure.[74]

Race-Based Trauma Policies: Advocacy Groups Want More Action Taken

A number of advocacy groups have been outspoken on the issue of trauma. They want to do more than just have a conversation. They want to see more progress. For example, the advocacy organization called the California Campaign to Counter Childhood Adversity (4CA) is currently supporting a bill in the legislative cycle that will require children to be assessed for trauma as part of their routine health screening through Medicaid.[75] While there is a substantial amount of evidence that shows that trauma-informed policies should be implemented,[76] more than likely this bill will not pass because Democrats and Republications are deeply divided on health policy issues. Over the past few years, we have seen a tremendous spike in the number of heroin overdoses, especially in white neighborhoods.[77] Both Democrats and Republicans agree that we need to increase government spending on opioid addiction treatment. However, they have not come to the same conclusions when it comes to trauma-informed policies. For example, Republicans believe that we should strengthen existing programs that offer US troops counseling and treatment for trauma. However, they are only interested in this policy if states are willing to pay the bill.[78] Democrats would like to treat mental health issues, such as race-based trauma, with the same care we treat physical health issues. Democrats also realize that maintaining good mental health is good for all people, including people from vulnerable populations, ensuring that they have access to mental health care.[79]

The Policy of Delaware's Executive Order 24

To date, only a handful of policies address race-based trauma. The problem is that policy differs by state.[80] Delaware Governor John Carney signed Executive Order 24 in 2018, which mandates that all family services, both public and private, must create a "trauma awareness month," consisting of events for the community to engage in, and must develop a trauma-informed tool kit to help implement strategies for children and families exposed to race-based trauma.[81] While this is a first good step, it is not enough; policy makers are increasing the general knowledge and recognition of trauma, but they are not increasing the resources needed to treat trauma.

Success in the Middle Act of 2019

Policy makers introduced a Congressional bill called the Success in the Middle Act of 2019.[82] This bill focuses on providing middle school students with academic, social, and emotional support for trauma-informed care services so they can successfully progress to secondary and post-secondary education.[83] The problem with this bill is that it never mentions after-school programs. Therefore, when students are in school, they have the opportunity to receive services for their trauma. However, when they leave school and return home to their neighborhoods, they will once again be directly experiencing or witnessing race-based trauma. If the Success in the Middle Act of 2019 included after-school programs, then the bill would be giving students from low-income neighborhoods the opportunity to minimize their trauma by helping them to build resilience.

The Baltimore City Trauma-Responsive Care Act

In the city of Baltimore, policy makers introduced the Baltimore City Trauma-Responsive Care Act.[84] This bill is designed to build a trauma-informed workforce in schools, health care settings, social services, after-school programs, early childhood education, and the justice system. The first part of the bill focuses on youth who have been exposed to trauma. The second part of the bill focuses on other areas, such as expanding opportunities for art therapy and interventions for hospital-based trauma to prevent readmissions into hospitals for local and tribal families who have experienced high levels of trauma.[85] The problem with this bill is that it will increase the burden on these agencies and their staff. At agencies in the city of Baltimore, such as hospitals, social services, and health care settings, the staff are already overburdened and oftentimes struggling to accomplish day-to-day activities. Adding additional responsibilities to staff in many of these agencies will only create stress and impede the effective delivery of services to reduce trauma.[86]

Of course, trauma often carries a stigma. Just because policy makers implemented the act for agencies to help those who have experienced trauma, people in those communities will not automatically flock to these agencies. Research has shown that women who have suffered violence from their husbands or boyfriends tend to distrust city social workers.[87] The possibility remains that these city employees will unintentionally disclose information about the trauma these women experienced, causing the women to be stigmatized in their own community.

Policy makers seem to be confused when it comes to addressing race-based trauma and the impact it has on people of color. While they generally understand that this form of trauma is passed down from one generation to the next, they fear that acknowledging this fact means that there are gaps in learning and health outcomes for children and families who experience and witness trauma. I believe that this is something that they don't want to deal with, politically or morally. Politically, policy makers would have to provide an abundance of resources to all of the agencies in Baltimore—schools, health care agencies, social services, after-school programs, early childhood centers, and the justice system—which would require large amounts of funding from taxpayers of the city of Baltimore. From a moral standpoint, if policy makers recognize that race-based trauma does impact people of color, then policy makers would have to acknowledge their own privilege and complicity, something they are not willing to do anytime soon.

Conclusion

It's easy to point the finger at technology, mass media, traumatic events, and the closing of at-risk hospitals for all of the health disparities that we see in low-income urban neighborhoods across the country. However, based on my work as a researcher, this is what we should expect when we do not have health policies that take into consideration the conditions of the most vulnerable in our society. No one wants to be isolated in this world, without any means of communication, especially when technology exists that can keep us connected.

Similarly, no one wants to live in low-income neighborhoods where they experience and witness trauma on an everyday basis. I can say without hesitation that it is not something that I want for my friends, the people in my neighborhood, myself, or my family. I would not even want it for my worst enemy. I hope I never have to look over my shoulder when I walk home at night.

In Birmingham, Alabama, where the Worley family lives, it's not uncommon to see drive-by shootings or people hanging out on the street corner at all hours of the night, or having arguments in the streets. Yet, in the midst of all this trauma, the Worleys' family unit is intact. They don't have to sleep in a homeless shelter, or on some bench in the park. They have a life and they have each other, even though it is not perfect. This place is their home.

The key is not to knock people down who live in low-income urban neighborhoods, but to find ways to build them up, and to make sure people living in poverty no longer accept the ideology that the reason why they are in the position that they are in is because they have put themselves there and have chosen this way of life.

Notes

1. Thimbleby, "Technology and the Future of Healthcare."
2. Thimbleby, "Technology and the Future of Healthcare."
3. Tobin-Tyler and Teitelbaum, *Essentials of Health Justice*, 10–13.
4. Thompson, "NYPD's Infamous Stop-and-Frisk Policy."
5. Currie, "Positive and Negative Constitutional Rights."
6. Norman, "District Court Ruling."
7. Murphy Paul, "Is Technology Widening Opportunity Gaps?'
8. Murphy Paul, "Is Technology Widening Opportunity Gaps?"
9. Stevens, "History of Television."
10. "Television in the 1990s."
11. Stevens, "History of Television."
12. "Television in the 1990s."
13. "Television in the 1990s."
14. Jan, "News Media."
15. Jan, "News Media."
16. Jan, "News Media."
17. Jan, "News Media."
18. Jan, "News Media."
19. Jan, "News Media."
20. Champa, "Misinformation in the Media."
21. Hsia, Kellermann, and Shen, "Factors Associated with Closures."
22. Burkey et al., "Impact of Hospital Closures."
23. Doyle and Cresswell, "What Was Healthcare?"
24. Doyle and Cresswell, "What Was Healthcare?"
25. St. Vincent's Hospital Manhattan was founded in 1849 and is the third oldest hospital in New York City. The hospital was the epicenter of the AIDS epidemic in New York City and one of the first institutions to address HIV/AIDS. It also was the primary admitting hospital for the victims of the September 11 attacks on the World Trade Center and the Pentagon.

26. See footnote 28.

27. Harvey Wingfield, "Disproportionate Impact of Covid-19."

28. Delaware Health and Social Services, "Emily P. Bissell Hospital."

29. Ellison, "3 Obvious."

30. Carson et al., "Effects of Small Hospital Closure."

31. Carson et al., "Effects of Small Hospital Closure."

32. Ellison, "3 Obvious."

33. Ellison, "3 Obvious."

34. Shepard, "UAB Health System."

35. Daily Briefing, "Rural Hospitals Keep Closing."

36. Daily Briefing, "Rural Hospitals Keep Closing."

37. Miller, "When Work Moves."

38. Clark, "Tulsa's 'Black Wall Street.'"

39. Clark, "Tulsa's 'Black Wall Street.'"

40. Chang, "Massacre of Black Wall Street."

41. Clark, "Tulsa's 'Black Wall Street.'"

42. Clark, "Tulsa's 'Black Wall Street.'"

43. Clark, "Tulsa's 'Black Wall Street.'"

44. Miller, "When Work Moves."

45. Miller, "When Work Moves."

46. Miller, "When Work Moves."

47. Lacy, *Blue-Chip Black*.

48. *U.S. News & World Report*, "HBCU Rankings 2022."

49. Burton, "Spelman College No. 1 HBCU."

50. Lee and Kaleem, "Historically Black Colleges Struggle."

51. Jacobs, "Unprecedented Crisis."

52. Lee and Kaleem, "Historically Black Colleges Struggle."

53. Slater, "Blacks Who First Entered."

54. Deville, "Historically Black Colleges."

55. Goldmann et al., "Pervasive Exposure to Violence."

56. Goldmann et al., "Pervasive Exposure to Violence."

57. Craigie, Grawert, and Kimble, "Conviction, Imprisonment, and Lost Earnings."

58. Martin, "Hidden Consequences."

59. Martin, "Hidden Consequences."

60. Martin, "Hidden Consequences."

61. Martin, "Hidden Consequences."

62. Motley and Banks, "Black Males."

63. The National Crime Victimization Survey is the nation's primary source of information on criminal victimization and has been collecting data since 1973. The survey is the largest forum in which victims can describe the impact of crime on their lives and the characteristics of their violent offenders.

64. Motley and Banks, "Black Males."

65. Motley and Banks, "Black Males."

66. Perez, "It's Not Just Black and White People."

67. Williams, "Black Communities Suffer Trauma."

68. Williams, "Black Communities Suffer Trauma."

69. Ross, "Impacts of Historical Trauma."

70. Ross, "Impacts of Historical Trauma."

71. Ross, "Impacts of Historical Trauma."

72. Blackwell and Ford, "Latino Immigrants."

73. Blackwell and Ford, "Latino Immigrants."

74. Blackwell and Ford, "Latino Immigrants."

75. The California Campaign to Counter Childhood Adversity (4CA) has led efforts to mitigate the effects of childhood toxic stress through the creation of a statewide policy in California. To date, they have increased awareness about childhood trauma in the areas of education, health, and youth justice.

76. See footnote 78.

77. Alexander, Kiang, and Barbieri, "Black and White Opioid Mortality."

78. Republican Party Platform, "Supporting Our Troops."

79. American Presidency Project, "2016 Democratic Party Platform."

80. Schulman, "Policy Update."

81. Carney, "Governor Carney Signs Executive Order."

82. US Senator Sheldon Whitehouse of Rhode Island and Representative Raúl Grijalva of Arizona introduced the Success in the Middle Act of 2019 to give schools resources to improve the graduation rates of at-risk youth. This bill is based on the proportion of children experiencing poverty in a given school.

83. See footnote 85.

84. The Baltimore City Trauma-Responsive Care Act was renamed the Elijah Cummings Healing City Act to honor the late Congressman Cummings in his ongoing efforts to address childhood trauma.

85. McArdle and Rubens, "Baltimore City Trauma Responsive Care Act."

86. McArdle and Rubens, "Baltimore City Trauma Responsive Care Act."

87. McArdle and Rubens, "Baltimore City Trauma Responsive Care Act."

Bibliography

Alexander, Monica J., Mathew V. Kiang, and Magali Barbieri. "Trends in Black and White Opioid Mortality in the United States, 1979–2015." *Epidemiology* 29, no. 5 (2018): 707–15. https://doi.org/10.1097/EDE.0000000000000858.

American Presidency Project. "2016 Democratic Party Platform." Last updated July 21, 2016. https://www.presidency.ucsb.edu/documents/2016-democratic -party-platform.

Blackwell, Amanda, and Debra Ford. "Latino Immigrants: Experiences of Trauma and Barriers to Mental Health." *Mental Health*, 2 (2009): 1, 3–5.

Burkey, Mark L., J. Bhadury, H. A. Eiselt, and H. Toyoglu. "The Impact of Hospital Closures on Geographical Access: Evidence from Four Southeastern States of the United States." *Operations Research Perspectives*, 4 (2017): 56–66. https://doi.org/10.1016/j.orp.2017.03.003.

Burton, Jazmyn. "U.S. News & World Report: Spelman College No. 1 HBCU, Top 10 for Social Mobility and Innovation." Spelman College. Accessed October 15, 2021. https://www.spelman.edu/about-us/news-and-events/news-releases/2021/09/13/u.s.-news-world-report-spelman-college-no.-1-hbcu-top-10-for-social-mobility-and-innovation.

Carney, John. "Governor Carney Signs Executive Order Making Delaware a Trauma-Informed State." *Delaware News*. October 17, 2018. https://news.delaware.gov/2018/10/17/governor-carney-signs-executive-order-making-delaware-trauma-informed-state/.

Carson, Susan, Kim Peterson, Linda Humphrey, and Mark Helfand. "Evidence Brief: Effects of Small Hospital Closure on Patient Health Outcomes." *VA Evidence Synthesis Program Reports* (2013): 1–8.

Champa, Jared. "Misinformation in the Media and its Influence on Racism." Honors undergraduate thesis, University of Central Florida, 2021. https://stars.library.ucf.edu/honorstheses/880.

Chang, Natalie. "The Massacre of Black Wall Street." *Atlantic Re:think*. Accessed January 16, 2020. https://www.theatlantic.com/sponsored/hbo-2019/the-massacre-of-black-wall-street/3217/.

Clark, Alexis. "Tulsa's 'Black Wall Street' Flourished as a Self-Contained Hub in Early 1900s." History Channel. Last updated January 27, 2021. https://www.history.com/news/black-wall-street-tulsa-race-massacre.

Craigie, Terry-Ann, Ames Grawert, and Cameron Kimble. "Conviction, Imprisonment, and Lost Earnings: How Involvement with the Criminal Justice System Deepens Inequality." Brennan Center for Justice at New York University School of Law. Last updated September 15, 2020. https://www.brennancenter.org/sites/default/files/2020-09/Conviction_Imprisonment_and_Lost_Earnings.pdf.

Currie, David P. "Positive and Negative Constitutional Rights." *University of Chicago Law Review* 53, no. 3 (1986): 864–90.

Daily Briefing. "Rural Hospitals Keep Closing—And That Could Have Significant Health Effects." Advisory Board. Last updated November 19, 2018. https://www.advisory.com/daily-briefing/2018/11/19/rural-hospitals.

Delaware Health and Social Services. "State Will Close Emily P. Bissell Hospital Permanently." Delaware News (Delaware.gov). Last updated September 22, 2015. https://news.delaware.gov/2015/09/22/state-will-close-emily-p-bissell-hospital-permanently/.

Deville, Nancy. "Historically Black Colleges Try to Change with Times." *USA Today News*. August 19, 2013. https://www.usatoday.com/story/news/nation/2013/08/19/march-on-washington-hbcus-change/2646689/.

Doyle, Barry, and Rosemary Cresswell. "What Was Healthcare Like Before the NHS?" *Conversation* (Waltham, MA). July 3, 2018. http://theconversation.com/what-was-healthcare-like-before-the-nhs-99055.

Ellison, Ayla. "3 Obvious and Not-So-Obvious Reasons Hospitals Close." Becker's Hospital Review. Last updated May 18, 2016. https://www.beckershospitalreview.com/finance/3-obvious-and-not-so-obvious-reasons-hospital-close.html.

Goldmann, Emily, Allison Aiello, Monica Uddin, Jorge Delva, Karestan Koenen, Larry M. Gant, and Sandro Galea. "Pervasive Exposure to Violence and Posttraumatic Stress Disorder in a Predominantly African American Urban Community: The Detroit Neighborhood Health Study." *Journal of Traumatic Stress* 24, no. 6 (2011): 747–51. https://doi.org/10.1002/jts.20705.

Govtrack. "H.R. 3089 (116th): Success in the Middle Act of 2019." Accessed May 6, 2020. https://www.govtrack.us/congress/bills/116/hr3089/studyguide.

Harvey Wingfield, Adia. "The Disproportionate Impact of Covid-19 on Black Health Care Workers in the U.S." *Harvard Business Review*. May 14, 2020. https://hbr.org/2020/05/the-disproportionate-impact-of-covid-19-on-black-health-care-workers-in-the-u-s.

Hopkinson, Ashley. "Addressing Early Childhood Trauma Requires Shift in Policy, More Training for Teachers." *EdSource* (Oakland, CA). September 26, 2017. https://edsource.org/2017/addressing-early-childhood-trauma-requires-shift-in-policy-more-training-for-teachers/587756.

Hsia, Renee Y., Arthur L. Kellermann, and Yu-Chu Shen. "Factors Associated with Closures of Emergency Departments in the United States." *JAMA* 305, no. 19 (2011): 1978–85. https://doi.org/10.1001/jama.2011.620.

Jacobs, Peter. "There's an Unprecedented Crisis Facing America's Historically Black Colleges." *Insider* (New York, NY). March 30, 2015. https://www.businessinsider.com/hbcus-may-be-more-in-danger-of-closing-than-other-schools-2015-3.

Jan, Tracy. "News Media Offers Consistently Warped Portrayals of Black Families, Study Finds." *Washington Post*. December 13, 2017. https://www.washingtonpost.com/news/wonk/wp/2017/12/13/news-media-offers-consistently-warped-portrayals-of-black-families-study-finds/.

Lacy, Karyn. *Blue-Chip Black: Race, Class, and Status in the New Black Middle Class*. Berkeley, CA: University of California Press, 2007.

Lee, Kurtis, and Jaweed Kaleem. "As Historically Black Colleges Struggle, Bennett College for Women Fights to Stay Afloat." *Los Angeles Times*. April 22, 2019. https://www.latimes.com/nation/la-na-hbcu-historically-black-colleges-universities-north-carolina-bennett-college-20190422-htmlstory.html.

Martin, Eric. "Hidden Consequences: The Impact of Incarceration on Dependent Children." *National Institute of Justice Journal*, 278 (2017): 1–7. https://nij.ojp.gov/topics/articles/hidden-consequences-impact-incarceration-dependent-children.

McArdle, Flannery, and Kimberly Rubens. "Subject | 19–0410 The Baltimore City Trauma Responsive Care Act." Bill synopsis. July 22, 2019. http://healingcitybaltimore.com/mt-content/uploads/2019/12/draft_trauma-responsive-care-act.pdf.

Miller, Conrad. "When Work Moves: Job Suburbanization and Black Employment." *National Bureau of Economic Research* 60, no. 12 (2018): 1–49. http://www.nber.org/papers/w24728.

Motley, Robert, and Andrae Banks. "Black Males, Trauma, and Mental Health Service Use: A Systematic Review." *Perspectives on social work: the journal of the doctoral students of the University of Houston Graduate School of Social Work* 14, no. 1 (2018): 4–19.

Murphy Paul, Annie. "Is Technology Widening Opportunity Gaps Between Rich and Poor Kids?" *KQED* (San Francisco, CA). June 27, 2014. https://www.kqed.org/mindshift/36537/is-technology-widening-opportunity-gaps-between-rich-and-poor-kids.

Norman, Jane. "District Court Ruling Finds Individual Mandate Unconstitutional." *The Commonwealth Fund* (New York, NY). December 13, 2010. https://www.commonwealthfund.org/publications/newsletter-article/district-court-ruling-finds-individual-mandate-unconstitutional.

Perez, Maria. "It's Not Just Black and White People: Police Shootings Are Killing Latinos." *Newsweek*. September 23, 2017. https://www.newsweek.com/latinos-police-shootings-oklahoma-city-669854.

Purtle, Jonathan, and Michael Lewis. "Mapping 'Trauma-Informed' Legislative Proposals in U.S. Congress." *Administration and Policy in Mental Health* 44, no. 6 (2017): 867–76. https://doi.org/10.1007/s10488-017-0799-9.

Republican Party Platform. "Supporting Our Troops: Standing by Our Heroes." Accessed April 16, 2022. https://www.presidency.ucsb.edu/documents/2016-republican-party-platform.

Ross, Keisha. "Impacts of Historical Trauma and Its Effects on Health Seeking Behaviors for Communities of Color." Cultural Perspectives: Cedar Valley Mental Health Summit. September 13, 2019. https://www.hawkeyecollege.edu/webres/File/business-community/impacts-historical-trauma.pdf.

Rugh, Peter. "NYC's Vanishing Hospitals." *Indypendent* (Brooklyn, NY). April 4, 2014. https://indypendent.org/2014/04/nycs-vanishing-hospitals/.

Schulman, Meryl. "Policy Update: State and Federal Movement to Advance Trauma-Informed Care." Center for Healthcare Strategies. Last updated November 15, 2018. https://www.chcs.org/policy-update-state-and-federal-movement-to-advance-trauma-informed-care/.

Shepard, Bob. "UAB Health System, Ascension St. Vincent's Develop Strategic Alliance for Better Health." *UAB News* (Birmingham, AL). January 22, 2020. https://www.uab.edu/news/health/item/11047-uab-health-system-ascension-st-vincent-s-develop-strategic-alliance-for-better-health.

Slater, Robert Bruce. "The Blacks Who First Entered the World of White Higher Education." *Journal of Blacks in Higher Education*, no. 4 (1994): 47–56. https://doi.org/10.2307/2963372.

Stevens, Mitchell. "History of Television." *Grolier Encyclopedia* (Danbury, CT), 2000 edition. https://stephens.hosting.nyu.edu/History of Television page .html.

"Television in the 1990s." https://mentalitch.com/television-in-the-1990s/.

Thimbleby, Harold. "Technology and the Future of Healthcare." *Journal of Public Health Research* 2, no. 3 (2013): 160–67. https://dx.doi.org/10 .4081%2Fjphr.2013.e28.

Thompson, Taahira. "NYPD's Infamous Stop-and-Frisk Policy Found Unconstitutional." *Civil and Human Rights News.* Updated August 21, 2013. https:// civilrights.org/edfund/resource/nypds-infamous-stop-and-frisk-policy-found -unconstitutional/#.

Tobin-Tyler, Elizabeth, and Joel B. Teitelbaum. "The 'Negative Constitution.'" In *Essentials of Health Justice: A Primer*, 10–13. Burlington, MA: Jones and Bartlett Learning, 2019.

U.S. News & World Report. "HBCU Rankings 2022: The Top 25 Black Colleges from U.S. News." Last updated March 4, 2022. https://hbculifestyle.com/top -25-hbcu-rankings-2022/.

Williams, Tasha. "Research Shows Entire Black Communities Suffer Trauma After Police Shootings." *YES! Magazine.* August 3, 2018. https://www .yesmagazine.org/health-happiness/2018/08/03/research-shows-entire-black -communities-suffer-trauma-after-police-shootings/.

six

The Government's Programs and Role in Affecting and Protecting Our Health

IN 1996, President Bill Clinton and the US Congress created a program called Temporary Assistance for Needy Families (TANF) to replace the Aid to Families with Dependent Children (AFDC) program.[1] That program, founded in 1935, was a way to help single mothers living in poverty take care of their children by receiving cash welfare during a time when the US economy experienced the largest economic downturn in history. A number of researchers had claimed that the AFDC needed to be replaced because the program was creating a "culture of dependency" by those who used it during the Great Depression.[2] The main objective of TANF was to end entitlements for cash assistance for low-income families; rather, the federal government would provide block grants to the states, and states would determine who was eligible for benefits and services. The TANF program became an instant hit and one of Clinton's brightest moments during his presidency. Many Americans were relieved that people were no longer getting "free rides" for not wanting to work.[3]

Drawbacks of Temporary Assistance for Needy Families (TANF)

At some point, the role of our government in protecting and improving the health status of our most vulnerable citizens has shifted from helping needy families to wanting people to pull themselves up by their bootstraps—when they do not have any shoestrings—despite the barriers that have been placed in front of them and their families. The reality of TANF is that many of the services that it provides to low-income families come with drawbacks that precipitate negative health outcomes. For the past two decades, the funding for the TANF block grant has remained roughly the same: around $16.5 billion dollars a year, without any increases to account for population growth or inflation.[4] Since the program began in 1996, the program has not been able to adequately protect families from neediness and poverty when they fall on hard times.[5] Originally, eight out of 10 families that were living below the federal poverty level were able to receive assistance. Today, only one in three families receive help from TANF.[6] I believe the amount of federal money did not increase as much as it needed to. Even more depressing is that fewer than one in five families experiencing poverty receive TANF in more than half of all states, which can be contributed to more people living in poverty and cuts to and tighter restrictions on TANF benefits.[7]

TANF has proven to be unreliable in an economic downturn. When the Great Recession hit, unemployment soared and the number of families needing government help skyrocketed. TANF enjoyed some success in its early years when the economy was strong, but when the economy weakened, TANF failed to provide employee assistance and cash benefits to many families in need. As of a matter of fact, the number of families that received help from TANF actually dropped in many states.[8] As a researcher, this makes me question whether TANF is helping to support job readiness and independence by doing away with welfare, or continuing a cycle of keeping individuals who live in extreme poverty in a hopeless situation.

Because the money allocated by TANF has fallen overwhelmingly in value, it does very little to help families escape "deep poverty." Parents relying 100% on TANF to provide the basics for their children, during a time when they are unemployed, suffer from an illness, or are on disability, have less money to spend today than they did back in 2005. For example, in Ohio, for every 100 children in deep poverty, 54 received TANF benefits in 2005–2009, compared to 43 children receiving benefits in 2010–2014.[9] Researchers have reported that over half of Americans are at risk of experiencing poverty at some point during their adulthood.[10] I believe that our government needs to invest in providing the necessary protections against the ups and downs in life by strengthening the TANF program to help struggling families live a life that they not only want but deserve.

Social Security Disability Insurance Program

Another example of this kind of change in government programs is the Social Security Disability Insurance program.[11] Although President Dwight D. Eisenhower officially signed the Social Security Disability Insurance program into law in 1956, the changes that led up to this creation started much earlier.[12] In the early eighteenth century, about 73 to 80% of people worked in agriculture.[13] Most people took care of their basic needs by working on the land, not for a salary or an hourly wage. As long as you could grow food and keep your house maintained and functioning, you could provide for yourself and your family. Today, with the high costs of buying a home or renting an apartment, purchasing food, and increasing public transportation fares in urban cities, we see more susceptibility to poverty.[14] Unfortunately, some individuals are unable to work due to a disability; oftentimes they don't have the extra income or family resources to support them, causing that individual to fall into destitution. The Social Security Disability Insurance program was not the first program to address the ills of people who are unable to work due to a disability. In 1934, Huey Long revealed his Share Our Wealth plan, in which he offered a stipend to help families earning less than one-third of the national average income—enough money so that they could buy a home, automobile, and radio.[15] In addition, Long was an advocate for economic equity. During the 1930s, he believed that the collapse of the economy was a result of the vast disparity between the super-rich and everyone else.[16] The Social Security Disability Insurance program is unique because it is a federal initiative, not a state initiative or a welfare initiative. To receive Social Security Disability Insurance benefits, a person must meet the criteria based on their work history and how much income they have contributed to the Social Security Trust Fund through payroll or self-employment taxes. The individual must also prove that at no point do they have the capacity to work under any circumstances, for any period of time, due to a mental or physical impairment that has lasted or can be expected to last for a continuous period of not less than 12 months or to result in death.[17]

President Eisenhower's entire Social Security Disability Insurance program has changed and drifted far away from its original purpose. Senior research fellow at George Mason University Veronique de Rugy points out that the Social Security Disability Insurance program is damaged and financially unsustainable. She argues that when unemployment rises, applications for disability benefits also tend to rise, suggesting to some degree that the Social Security Disability Insurance program has become less of a protection for those with disabilities and more of an optional unemployment or welfare program.[18] In addition, David Autor, an economist and professor of economics at the Massachusetts Institute of Technology, argues that the Social Security Disability Insurance program does not give benefits for partial disability, and that benefits do not begin until after a recipient has lived with their disability for at least five full months. This means that they will not receive benefits until their sixth month, if not longer.[19]

Another flaw of the Social Security Disability Insurance program is the governmental barriers that cause significant hardships for adults living with a disability and in poverty. If a person's overall income is over a certain amount, then their benefits are taxable. For individuals, that amount is $25,000; for couples, it is $32,000.[20] Every year, approximately one-third of Social Security Disability Insurance recipients pay taxes on their benefits.[21] Paying taxes on their benefits can be a significant hardship for individuals with disabilities who don't have any other source of income.

I have researched and witnessed the impact of policies and legal doctrines on low-income neighborhoods for a long time, and I have learned to be cautious of the way our government operates. For example, I see our government making an effort to reduce disparities by helping families living in poverty, and then turning around and denying the same group of people income support, health insurance, housing assistance, and access to legal assistance. This can be seen with programs such as Medicaid, Medicare, public housing, and the right to counsel in legal matters.

Medicaid

Medicaid was created in 1965, as part of the Social Security Amendments, by President Lyndon B. Johnson to address the war on poverty.[22] The program was designed to provide health insurance for those living in poverty and with disabilities, who otherwise could not afford or have access to health insurance.[23] Medicaid has always been successful when the federal and state governments work together. Since it is an entitlement program, all individuals who meet federal and state criteria are eligible for guaranteed coverage.[24] Medicaid now covers over 76 million Americans.[25] In addition to providing health coverage to those experiencing poverty and those with disabilities, Medicaid is a major contributor to the US health care system, accounting for about 17% of the national health care spending in a calendar year.[26] This includes community health centers, hospitals, nurse practitioners, nursing homes, physicians, and other health professionals.[27]

However, I argue that the same Medicaid program that finances a large portion of the health care system is the same program by which the federal government has limited the amount of coverage people living in poverty can receive, due to federal budget cuts over time. In the summer of 2017, Republicans proposed to change Medicaid from an entitlement program to a block grant.[28] In addition, many states have proposed that in order to receive Medicaid coverage, there need to be work requirements for those experiencing poverty.[29] I should point out that these changes have been implemented, even though the criteria vary from state to state. The majority of the states have set the standard that people are required to work approximately 20 hours per week, or 80 hours a month, to receive Medicaid benefits.[30] To me, it appears that our government wants to determine who is deserving of their assistance, how much assistance should be provided to those who are disabled and/

or experiencing poverty, and if this assistance should come in the form of income support or through health care coverage.

Medicare

Medicare, like Medicaid, was created in 1965 to prevent vulnerable groups and people who are 65 years and older from not having access to health care. Medicare has no income requirements, and therefore is based on an individual's eligibility. Regarding Medicare, there is some bipartisanship amongst Democrats and Republican policy makers.[31] The biggest threat to Medicare is something many Americans have probably never heard of. Millions of seniors will be enrolled into a third-party program called Direct Contracting without their full knowledge or consent.[32] Direct Contracting allows commercial insurers and nonprofit organizations to manage the health of seniors, using a fee-for-service payment model. Instead of doctors and hospitals being paid directly for senior care, Direct Contracting will receive a monthly payment to cover a portion of senior medical expenses.[33] Let's not forget that they are allowed to keep what they don't spend on medical services.

Why is this bad for seniors? Basically, any type of company can apply to be a "Direct Contracting Entity"; this includes commercial insurers and capital investors.[34] What is really alarming is that applicants are approved without any oversight from Congress.[35] Furthermore, there are no requirements that Direct Contracting Entities have to be majority-owned by health care providers.[36] This leaves the door open to anyone in society, even companies with no health care experience at all.

When Donald Trump was president, he took executive action to suspend the collection of certain federal payroll taxes.[37] He also pledged that if re-elected, he will make permanent cuts to Medicare.[38] According to researchers, Trump's proposed cuts could exceed $2 trillion over 10 years, which would further weaken the nation's premier safety net during a time when Americans are more likely to need it the most.[39]

Medicare's primary beneficiaries, older adults, tend to have stronger political representation than those who receive Medicaid, which largely are our citizens in poverty and with disabilities.[40] However, I believe that at a pivotal time for health care in our nation, when many scholars are identifying problems that will have lasting impacts on the health of older adults by the year 2040, our government continues to ignore the issues that will ultimately create a shortfall for Medicare.

The first issue is that this program, which is predominantly designed to help older Americans pay for hospital and other outpatient services, is on pace to exhaust a good amount of cash that has been put in reserve by 2040.[41] The primary reason for this cash shortfall is that people are living longer than ever; the average life expectancy for a US citizen is 79 years of age.[42] This means that older adults who are eligible for Medicare are leaning on the program for longer periods of time than they did in the 1980s and early 1990s.[43] The second issue involves rising health care costs. I believe that new and innovative cancer drugs, robotic surgical tools, and personalized medicine are some of the reasons cash is being drained from Medicare's reserves, especially when health care costs are rising faster than inflation.

But the biggest obstacle facing Medicare is education, especially for older adults who reside in low-income urban neighborhoods and have less than a college education. The lack of effort from our government to ensure that older adults understand how Medicare works, as well as the differences between the original Medicare and Medicare Advantage, continues to prevent older adults with low incomes from making the best choice possible regarding their health plan.[44]

The original Medicare is a government-sponsored plan that consists of three primary parts: Part A, Part B, and Part D.[45] Part A, which is hospital insurance, helps cover costs related to hospital care, nursing facilities, and hospice care. Most people do not pay a premium with Part A.[46] Part B is supplementary medical insurance; this does have a premium, and it covers the physician and preventative services.[47] Part D is the prescription drug plan, which also carries a monthly premium.[48] The issue I see with Medicare is that it normally has a 20% out-of-pocket cost for older adults, but—crucially—this cost is not capped. Therefore, if someone needed an expensive cancer treatment, they could wind up paying a very costly health care bill that they most likely could not afford to pay. I think that Medicare is a poor program on the part of our government that keeps older adults with lower incomes living in poverty.

Medicare Advantage, or Part C

This brings us to Medicare Advantage, or Part C, which is insurance coverage offered by private insurance companies.[49] The problem I have with Medicare Advantage is that it is run and operated by private insurance companies, meaning people have less access to their choice of in-network providers. This is problematic because if an older adult suddenly became chronically ill, they might need to see a specialist that is out of network—but unfortunately, since private insurance companies want to control costs, they will not cover the person's bill, forcing them to pay out of pocket for those charges. As I see it, the real bottom line of this governmental program is that Medicare Advantage wants to keep older adults enrolled in their program as long as they remain healthy. However, if a person's health condition changes, they just might find out that they are no longer considered a valued member of Medicare Advantage. Calvin Whittredge offered his feelings about and experience with Medicare Advantage:

> I am not a fan of Medicare Advantage at all. I used to receive great care up until I became sick. A few weeks ago, I needed to see a specialist for my condition. When I received my bill, it turned out that I had to pay more than what I would have under my original Medicare plan. They told me that Medicare Advantage only covers certain doctors. If I had known that, I would have never went to the hospital and seen the specialist. . . . What gives them the right to limit my choice on which doctor I can and cannot see? I'm sick, and that's what should matter more than anything. But now they want me to pay extra for a doctor that is out of network, that no one told me about in the first place. I don't have money to pay for this bill.

This kind of treatment reveals a profound bias against older adults with lower incomes who live in urban neighborhoods, as they become chronically ill more often and do not have the finances to pay for health care services to out-of-network providers.

Public Housing Assistance Programs: Deterioration of People's Health through Evictions

The ability for individuals with low incomes and their families to be evicted from public housing assistance programs is another way in which I believe our government has allowed the health status of individuals living in poverty to deteriorate, particularly mothers and children. Since individuals experiencing poverty are required to sign a lease to live in public housing, this allows for the public housing authority to make all the rules and decide the consequences facing the tenants, who often do not have any protection.

When I visited the Colemans in Delaware, I asked Cynthia and Richard, "What was the most important service that they wanted the public housing authority to provide?" Both replied, "We want to live in public housing that does not endanger our quality of life and the health of our children." All public housing authorities have a rental office where tenants can go to file a complaint if the conditions they are living in are not up to housing code, which is required and mandated by the state. There were a few instances where the Colemans felt that their housing unit was in direct violation of the housing code. Cynthia stated,

> The window in my bedroom is painted shut and does not open. . . . I am constantly stressed and often worried that one day my apartment will catch on fire, causing me to be trapped in this apartment and possibly die from smoke inhalation. . . . I notified the housing authority, but nothing was ever done to fix the problem, and now I'm afraid that because I made a complaint to the rental office that my family will be targeted for eviction if I am ever late with my rent.

Many tenants living in poverty that file a complaint about their living conditions often fear that their landlord or public housing office will retaliate against them. For people with lower incomes, exercising their legal right to make a complaint against their landlord comes at a high cost. A number of states have laws to protect vulnerable groups from illegal evictions from their landlord or public housing authority. The first option is the tenant can receive a seven-day notice if they have not paid the rent when it was due. The tenant can remedy the situation by paying the rent within those seven days to stop the eviction all together. The second option is the landlord can give the tenant a 30-day notice to move out of the rental property if the landlord wants to end the rental agreement.[50]

Gideon v. Wainwright

By continuously separating criminal and civil legal services, our government has ensured that vulnerable groups do not have access to or cannot afford civil legal services to enforce their rights.

The government is required to provide legal counsel in criminal cases, both during trial and on appeal, to all defendants who are unable to afford a lawyer. The right to have a lawyer was first established on January 15, 1963, with *Gideon v. Wainwright*.[51] The case began with Clarence Gideon being charged in a Florida state court with breaking and entering. Gideon appeared in court without a lawyer, and requested that the court appoint one for him. The court did not appoint a lawyer for Gideon on the basis that it only appoints a lawyer to poverty-stricken defendants in capital cases. He was forced to represent himself in trial, where he was found guilty and sentenced to five years in prison. He later filed an appeal to the Supreme Court, arguing that the court's decision violated his constitutional right to be represented by an attorney. The Supreme Court agreed with Gideon and ruled in his favor, stating that "if desired, any poverty-stricken defendant has the right to have an attorney represent them in court and this is a guaranteed right under the U.S. Constitution."

Unfortunately, when it comes to civil cases, there is no law that guarantees a person assistance from a lawyer, even if the individual is poverty-stricken. Civil cases often involve issues such as age discrimination, religious beliefs, disability needs, educational discrimination, veteran health benefits, and lack of mental health services. By not providing an attorney in these civil suits, the government demonstrates that it is not willing to advocate and fight against systemic injustices.

Because many individuals with low incomes and their families cannot afford legal fees, many of them give up instead of fighting injustice in civil legal matters. The Community Needs and Services Study showed that two-thirds of adults in US cities have experienced one civil injustice in the past year.[52] Many of these civil injustices were reported by Black and Hispanic people living in poverty, who knew that the problem they were experiencing was legal in nature but did not have the financial means to hire an attorney to help them fight their disputes.

Earned Income Tax Credit

In April 2019, I was in New Orleans, Louisiana, presenting a paper at the 12th annual Health Disparities Conference at Xavier University, a Historically Black University.[53] There, I had a discussion with the director of the National Institute on Minority Health and Health Disparities, Dr. Eliseo J. Pérez-Stable. I wanted to know how our government could help in the fight to end severe poverty in low-income neighborhoods. In the midst of our conversation, other featured guest speakers at the conference, such as Patrice A. Harris, MD, the then president of the American Medical Association, and Oliver T. Brooks, MD, president of the National Medical Association, began talking about the importance of the Earned Income Tax Credit.

The Earned Income Tax Credit provides a significant amount of support to low- to moderate-income working families. Workers receive a credit equal to the percentage of their earnings up to a maximum credit. Both the credit rate and the maximum rate vary by family size—in other words, the more children a family has, the larger the credits they receive.[54] After the credit reaches its maximum, it remains flat until the family's earnings reach the credit phaseout point. At that point, it declines by each additional dollar of income until no credit is available. The primary goals of the Earned Income Tax credit are to reduce poverty and inspire, give confidence to, and reward families who want to work.[55]

By design, the Earned Income Tax Credit only benefits working families. In 2018, the maximum credit for families with one child was $3,461; for families with three or more children, the maximum credit was $6,431.[56] The Center on Budget and Policy Priorities is a non-profit organization that analyzes how federal and state budget policies can help low-income families afford the basics by advancing equity and reducing poverty.[57] The Earned Income Tax Credit has helped many Americans recover from the pandemic, and if Democrats and Republicans continue to work together as they did in 2021, the Earned Income Tax Credit will be an important step in making the American economy stronger.[58] It would benefit an estimated 17.4 million American workers, increasing their ability to pay rent, afford enough healthy food, and have access to health care.[59]

Supplemental Nutritional Assistance Program

The Supplemental Nutritional Assistance Program (SNAP) is a good example of how the government is protecting the health of many low-income families.[60] SNAP is an entitlement program that provides benefits to low-income families so they can purchase healthy, high-quality food. The amount of SNAP benefits a family receives depends on their income—for example, a family that has no income would qualify for the maximum amount of benefits.[61] SNAP is effective at addressing health disparities because the federal government and the states teamed up together to fund the SNAP program. At the federal level, the main responsibility of the government is to set the program's guidelines and support the states in administering the services. All of this is done through the US Department of Agriculture Food and Nutrition Service. The states' responsibilities are to educate the public, determine who in their state meets the criteria, and distribute SNAP to those families who are eligible. Nationwide, it is estimated that about 84% of food-insecure households participate in the SNAP program.[62]

This is a significant achievement, but the government is determined to do more to raise the profile of hunger and poverty. In 2021, the Biden administration revised the standard for food stamps and prompted the largest permanent increase to benefits in the program's history. This increase in benefits will reduce hunger, improve nutrition, and lead to better health for people who experience poverty.[63]

Fixing the Obesity Epidemic in Low-Income Urban Neighborhoods

Earlier this year, the American Medical Association urged physicians to screen children who reside in low-income urban neighborhoods and to identify the negative health outcomes associated with obesity and inadequate access to healthy food.[64] Data from the US Department of Agriculture also indicated that the highest number of unhealthy dietary food patterns exist in states with the largest communities of low-income housing.[65] Unhealthy eating has become an epidemic in low-income neighborhoods due to the fact that people are not meeting their recommended daily nutritional needs. In the United States, it is recommended that the average American diet should consist of 20 to 35 grams of fiber daily. However, many people only consume 12 to 17 grams of fiber in their daily diet.[66] As a society, we consume far more than the recommended daily allowance of sugar, fat, and salt.

Oftentimes, we make the assumption that the solution to "fixing" America's obesity epidemic and reducing health disparities in low-income urban neighborhoods is to increase the number of full-service supermarkets and grocery stores so that people living in poverty can have access to healthier foods. I believe that we have been bamboozled if we think this is the solution to solving our obesity problem, and that we must come to terms with the fact that the way we provide access to healthy food to people who live in low-income urban neighborhoods is broken. We must rethink this idea that just because healthy food choices such as fruits and vegetables are provided to supermarkets and grocery stores in low-income neighborhoods, more people in those neighborhoods will begin to consume greater amounts of fruits and vegetables and, as a result, health disparities around the issue of obesity will be reduced. For instance, a study conducted in Philadelphia, Pennsylvania, examined the impact of building a new supermarket in a low-income neighborhood. For just a few months after the supermarket's grand opening, a majority of the neighborhood used the new supermarket for shopping. When compared to another low-income neighborhood as a control group, the new supermarket maintained the perception that people in their neighborhood were eating healthier because they had access to a clean storefront and an orderly supermarket by advertising with new signs in front of the store. However, there was no evidence that neighborhood residents consumed more fruits and vegetables or had a healthier diet.[67]

The US government contends that obesity and unhealthy dieting can be a matter of life or death and that they need to be more creative with their policy initiatives—especially for people who live in low-income neighborhoods, as they are often hit the hardest by diet-related ailments such as heart disease and diabetes.[68] A study by researchers in Baltimore, Maryland, examined a rebate program for SNAP participants when purchasing healthy food. The study had a sample size of 622,793 (63.1% were African American and 28.2% were non-white Hispanics), and its participants received $0.35 in cash back for every dollar spent on fruits, vegetables, and non-sugary drinks. After the first year of the study, those who received the incentive reported consuming more fruits and vegetables and fewer sugary drinks per day.[69] I believe that incentivizing healthy food purchases from corner stores and local bodegas appears to be an effective policy for the SNAP program and has the potential to address obesity by helping individuals and their families make dietary changes.

But are these incentives enough? We don't yet know the health outcomes of such changes. We need to conduct more longitudinal studies to see the impact of these incentives. In fact, the last time I visited the Hughes family in the Bronx in New York City, I stopped by the local corner store and spoke with the storeowner, and learned that they were stocking their shelves with healthier food items such as fresh fruit, canned vegetables, and whole grains. However, when I asked the owner, "Have you noticed an increase in the number of healthy items being sold in your store since the incentives program was put into effect, and has it had any impact on the community?" The owner responded, "There have been a good number of people from the neighborhood buying fruits and vegetables from me . . . but I can't say with certainty how much impact this has had on the people in the neighborhood."

There are a number of independent scholars who are collaborating with the US government, making a conscious effort to influence politicians on both sides of the aisle to implement policies that protect the health of people in the United States, especially that of children. The Healthy, Hunger-Free Kids Act of 2010 sets policies for child nutrition programs. It was implemented in 2013–2014 and was aligned with the National School Lunch Program and the School Breakfast Program, and met the required dietary guidelines for Americans. The program emphasized fruits, vegetables, and whole grains, with the goal of reducing obesity.[70]

In 2014–2015, additional requirements came into effect, including healthier snacks and beverages sold outside of school meal plans.[71] School districts across the country are complaining that they are having a hard time implementing these new guidelines because of the rise in food prices and children throwing away the healthier food options. One school district reported that the changes in their lunches led to a three-week student boycott.[72] Despite the complaints by school districts across the nation and student unrest, the US government has remained committed to implementing the Healthy, Hunger-Free Kids Act of 2010. I cannot state definitively that the Healthy, Hunger-Free Kids Act of 2010 caused children to eat more fruits and vegetables and prompted a decline in obesity among children living in poverty. What I can state is that, based on research that I have conducted over the years and published in peer-reviewed journals such as *Journal of Public Health Policy, Journal of Public Affairs*, and the *Journal of Race and Policy,* I believe the Healthy, Hunger-Free Kids Act of 2010 is a law that should be strengthened, and built upon to help those living in poverty.

New Policies: Protecting the Health of People in Society

There are other policies that the US government is introducing to protect the public's health, listed below:

- Under Aidan's Law (H.R. 534), all newborns will be required to be screened for adrenoleukodystrophy (ALD), a brain disease that affects the central nervous system primarily in young boys and may lead to paralysis or death. In 2019, Aidan's Law was referred to the subcommittee of health. If passed, screening will be available in every US state to help reduce health disparities between people who don't have access to health care screening and people who do.[73]
- The Competitive Health Insurance Reform Act of 2020 (H.R. 1418) is a law that will encourage more open-market competition for health insurance. For years, the health insurance industry has been avoiding accountability under certain laws. In 2021, the bill became a law. It will help level the playing field between health insurers, providers, and consumers. This legislation will also help to make health insurance more affordable and decrease health disparities, especially for families with lower incomes.[74]
- The MORE Health Education Act (H.R. 987) is a bill that requires the Department of Health and Human Services to provide outreach and educational activities related to federal programs—for example, access to health insurance and less costly prescription drugs. This new bill, which was passed by Congress, helps reduce health disparities by addressing language barriers. All federal programs that provide access to health insurance and financial assistance for people in need are required to be culturally and linguistically easy to comprehend by their recipients.[75]
- The End Drunk Driving Act of 2019 (H.R. 3011) is a bill that was referred to the subcommittee on Consumer Protection and Commerce in 2019. It will require automobile manufacturers to develop alcohol detection technology to be installed in vehicles to prevent drunk driving. In the event that a driver gets behind the wheel of a car, the motor vehicle will not operate if the driver is under the influence of alcohol. If this bill is passed, the government will have the capacity to protect the health of and save over 59,000 lives over a 15-year period.[76]

- Recognizing the duty of the Federal Government to create a Green New Deal (H.Res. 109)[77] is a bill that was referred to the Subcommittee on Energy and Mineral Resources in 2019. The purpose of the bill is to provide economic stability for all people in the United States, securing clean air and water and access to healthy foods and promoting equality, equity, and justice. The bill has the potential to reduce health disparities by removing pollution and lessening greenhouse gas emissions, providing higher-quality health care, establishing higher-wage jobs, and providing safe, affordable housing to all, especially those who reside in low-income neighborhoods.

An Opportunity for the Government to Make Positive Changes

The United States government has the ability and the strength to make a lot of positive changes in our society when it comes to the health of its citizens. It can make laws, it can enforce laws, it can authorize amendments to the Constitution, and it can take measures for public health and safety. Why, then, is the government unable to eliminate health disparities? It could do that and still remain wealthy—or could it? The federal government lacks a national coordinated infrastructure that promotes and defends human rights, resulting in a lack of protection that varies from state to state. Furthermore, the government has gone back on its promise to guarantee effective measures to remedy discrimination on the basis of race and ethnicity in the area of health over the last decade. The United States government has an obligation not to ignore, defend, or support discrimination, but to review any governmental policies which may have the effect of continuing discrimination, and change their laws accordingly.

How, then, do we reduce health disparities in low-income urban neighborhoods? How do we get policy makers to implement new laws to improve public health for all, especially for families who live in poverty in urban neighborhoods? Despite some of the great strategies that the government has implemented, we still need to find ways to change the distribution of healthy environments, economic resources, and opportunities. This will ultimately require a fundamental shift in how policy is used to promote health. What can we do, individually, environmentally, nationally, and globally, to address disparities in low-income urban neighborhoods?

Notes

1. In its first few decades of existence, the Aid to Families with Dependent Children (AFDC) program had a provision in its law that it would only provide assistance to "suitable families"—meaning the child's parents had to be married. It prohibited assistance to "illegitimate" children whose father or mother was not married or absent from the home. See Tobin-Tyler and Teitelbaum, *Essentials of Health Justice*, 97–98.
2. Spalding, "Culture of Dependency." See also Tobin-Tyler and Teitelbaum, *Essentials of Health Justice*, 97–98.
3. Office of Family Assistance, "What We Do."
4. Tobin-Tyler and Teitelbaum, *Essentials of Health Justice*, 97–98.
5. Tobin-Tyler and Teitelbaum, *Essentials of Health Justice*, 97–98.
6. Tobin-Tyler and Teitelbaum, *Essentials of Health Justice*, 97–98.
7. Tobin-Tyler and Teitelbaum, *Essentials of Health Justice*, 97–98.
8. Schott, "Why TANF Is Not a Model."
9. Britton and Luscheck, "Ohioans Living in Deep Poverty."
10. Confronting Poverty, "Poverty Facts and Myths."
11. The Social Security Disability Insurance program does not just focus on people who are unable to work due to physical illness. There are also "invisible disabilities" that are unseen but equally covered under the program. These conditions include diabetes, chronic fatigue syndrome, bipolar disorder, anxiety, post-traumatic stress disorder, epilepsy, and schizophrenia. See Kearney, "Social Security and the 'D' in OASDI."
12. Kearney, "Social Security."
13. Lebergott, "Labor Force and Employment."
14. Dickler, "Home Prices"; Winters, "Rising Inflation"; Jaffe, "Mass Transit Fares."
15. The Share Our Wealth plan was introduced by Huey Long in 1934. The program was designed to provide a decent standard of living to all Americans. Long advocated for free education, health benefits for the elderly, and a yearly stipend for all families living below the national poverty level. See Long, "Share Our Wealth."
16. Long, "Share Our Wealth."

17. Tobin-Tyler and Teitelbaum, *Essentials of Health Justice*, 98–99.

18. de Rugy, "Social Security Disability Insurance."

19. David Autor is one of the leading labor economists in the world and an internationally recognized authority on how technological change, globalization, and trade agreements affect labor markets, who also researches what causes inequality. See also Tobin-Tyler and Teitelbaum, *Essentials of Health Justice*, 98–99.

20. Laurence, "Are Social Security Benefits Taxed?"

21. Laurence, "Are Social Security Benefits Taxed?"

22. Tobin-Tyler and Teitelbaum, *Essentials of Health Justice*, 100.

23. Tobin-Tyler and Teitelbaum, *Essentials of Health Justice*, 100.

24. Tobin-Tyler and Teitelbaum, *Essentials of Health Justice*, 100.

25. Pradhan, "Millions on Medicaid are at Risk."

26. Tobin-Tyler and Teitelbaum, *Essentials of Health Justice*, 100.

27. Rudowitz and Hinton, "10 Things to Know."

28. Tobin-Tyler and Teitelbaum, *Essentials of Health Justice*, 100.

29. Tobin-Tyler and Teitelbaum, *Essentials of Health Justice*, 100.

30. American Academy of Family Physicians, "Medicaid Work Requirements."

31. Jayapal and Rogers, "Biggest Threat to Medicare."

32. Jayapal and Rogers, "Biggest Threat to Medicare."

33. Jayapal and Rogers, "Biggest Threat to Medicare."

34. Jayapal and Rogers, "Biggest Threat to Medicare."

35. Jayapal and Rogers, "Biggest Threat to Medicare."

36. Jayapal and Rogers, "Biggest Threat to Medicare."

37. Cohen, "Defund Social Security and Medicare?"

38. Cohen, "Defund Social Security and Medicare?"

39. Cohen, "Defund Social Security and Medicare?"

40. Tobin-Tyler and Teitelbaum, *Essentials of Health Justice*, 100–101.

41. Potter, "Medicare Advantage—or DISAdvantage?"

42. Ortaliza et al., "U.S. Life Expectancy."

43. Potter, "Medicare Advantage—or DISAdvantage?"

44. Rose, "Medicare and Medicaid."

45. Tobin-Tyler and Teitelbaum, *Essentials of Health Justice*, 100–101.

46. Tobin-Tyler and Teitelbaum, *Essentials of Health Justice*, 100–101.

47. Tobin-Tyler and Teitelbaum, *Essentials of Health Justice*, 100–101.

48. Tobin-Tyler and Teitelbaum, *Essentials of Health Justice*, 100–101.

49. Tobin-Tyler and Teitelbaum, *Essentials of Health Justice*, 100–101.

50. O'Connell, "How to Delay an Eviction."

51. Gideon v. Wainwright, 732 U.S. 335 (1963). See Tobin-Tyler and Teitelbaum, *Essentials of Health Justice*, 13–14.

52. Sandefur, "Accessing Justice."

53. The annual Health Disparities Conference, held at Xavier University, first began with a focus on diabetes-related illnesses. The focus expanded to include

health disparities, health equity, and bringing together national and international scholars to improve health outcomes in underserved populations. See Xavier University, "12th Annual Health Disparities Conference."

54. Tobin-Tyler and Teitelbaum, *Essentials of Health Justice*, 99.

55. Tobin-Tyler and Teitelbaum, *Essentials of Health Justice*, 99.

56. "Earned Income Tax Credit."

57. State Budget and Tax, "Policy Basics."

58. Shah, "Strong Earned Income Tax Credit."

59. Shah, "Strong Earned Income Tax Credit."

60. The Supplemental Nutritional Assistance Program (SNAP), formerly called the Food Stamps Program, was created to purchase food for low-income populations. See Tobin-Tyler and Teitelbaum, *Essentials of Health Justice*, 103–104.

61. Tobin-Tyler and Teitelbaum, *Essentials of Health Justice*, 103–104.

62. Tobin-Tyler and Teitelbaum, *Essentials of Health Justice*, 103–104.

63. DeParle, "Increase in Food Stamps."

64. John van Salee de Grasse was the first African American to gain admittance to any medical society in the United States. See Stein Berman et al., "Screening for Poverty."

65. Golan et al., "Low-Income Americans."

66. Wallace, "Health Disparities."

67. Chrisinger, "Mixed-Method Assessment."

68. Hurt et al., "Obesity Epidemic."

69. Lagisetty et al., "Baltimore City Virtual Supermarket Program."

70. Kenney et al., "Impact of Healthy, Hungry-Free Kids Act."

71. Kenney et al., "Impact of Healthy, Hungry-Free Kids Act."

72. McLaughlin, "New Federal School Lunch Rules."

73. Aidan's Law, H.R. 534, 116th Cong. (2019).

74. Competitive Health Insurance Reform Act of 2020, H.R. 1418, 116th Cong. (2021).

75. MORE Health Education Act, H.R. 987, 116th Cong. (2021).

76. End Drunk Driving Act of 2019, H.R. 3011, 116th Cong. (2019).

77. Recognizing the duty of the Federal Government to create a Green New Deal, H.Res. 109, 116th Con. (2019).

Bibliography

Aidan's Law, H.R. 534, 116th Cong. (2019). https://www.congress.gov/bill /116th-congress/house-bill/534?s=1&r=18.

American Academy of Family Physicians. "Medicaid Work Requirements." Last updated November 2022. https://www.aafp.org/dam/AAFP/documents /advocacy/coverage/medicaid/BKG-MedicaidWorkRequirements.pdf.

Britton, Tara, and Brie Luscheck. "Majority of Ohioans Living in Deep Poverty Don't Receive Cash Assistance: Temporary Assistance for Needy Families in Ohio." The Center for Community Solutions. Last updated October 1, 2018. https://www.communitysolutions.com/research/temporary-assistance-needy -families-ohio-balancing-program-integrity-entitlement-reducing-poverty-not -goal/.

Chrisinger, Benjamin. "A Mixed-Method Assessment of a New Supermarket in a Food Desert: Contributions to Everyday Life and Health." *Journal of Urban Health* 93, no. 3 (2016): 425–37. https://doi.org/10.1007/s11524-016-0055-8.

Cohen, Seth. "Defund Social Security and Medicare? Trump's Dangerous Attack on America's Safety Net." *Forbes.* August 10, 2020. https://www.forbes.com /sites/sethcohen/2020/08/10/defund-social-security-and-medicare-trumps -dangerous-attack-on-americas-safety-net/?sh=5719ba673410.

Competitive Health Insurance Reform Act of 2020, H.R. 1418, 116th Cong. (2021). https://www.congress.gov/bill/116th-congress/house-bill/1418/text.

Confronting Poverty. "Poverty Facts and Myths." Accessed April 15, 2022. https://confrontingpoverty.org/poverty-facts-and-myths/most-americans-will -experience-poverty/.

DeParle, Jason. "Biden Administration Prompts Largest Permanent Increase in Food Stamps." *New York Times.* August 15, 2021. https://www.nytimes.com /2021/08/15/us/politics/biden-food-stamps.html.

de Rugy, Veronique. "Social Security Disability Insurance Isn't Doing What It's Supposed to Do." Mercatus Center (George Mason University). September 23, 2015. https://www.mercatus.org/publications/government-spending/social -security-disability-insurance-isn%E2%80%99t-doing-what-it%E2%80%99s -supposed.

Dickler, Jessica. "Home Prices Are Now Rising Much Faster than Incomes, Studies Show." *CNBC News.* November 10, 2021. https://www.cnbc.com/2021/11/10 /home-prices-are-now-rising-much-faster-than-incomes-studies-show.html.

"The Earned Income Tax Credit: An Overview." Last updated January 12, 2021. https://www.everycrsreport.com/reports/R43805.html.

End Drunk Driving Act of 2019, H.R. 3011, 116th Cong. (2019). https://www .congress.gov/bill/116th-congress/house-bill/3011.

Golan, Elise, Hayden Stewart, Fred Kutchler, and Diansheng Dong. "Can Low-Income Americans Afford a Healthy Diet?" USDA Economic Research Service, US Department of Agriculture. Updated November 1, 2008. https:// www.ers.usda.gov/amber-waves/2008/november/can-low-income-americans -afford-a-healthy-diet/.

Hurt, Ryan T., Christopher Kulisek, Laura A. Buchanan, and Stephen A. McClave. "The Obesity Epidemic: Challenges, Health Initiatives, and Implications for Gastroenterologists." *Journal of Gastroenterology and Hepatology* 6, no. 12 (2010): 780–92. https://pubmed.ncbi.nlm.nih.gov /21301632/.

Jaffe, Eric. "The Real Reason Mass Transit Fares Are Rising Across the U.S." *Bloomberg*. April 4, 2014. https://www.bloomberg.com/news/articles/2014-04 -04/the-real-reason-mass-transit-fares-are-rising-across-the-u-s.

Jayapal, Pramila, and Susan Rogers. "The Biggest Threat to Medicare You've Never Even Heard Of." *The Hill*. December 9, 2021. https://thehill.com/blogs /congress-blog/healthcare/585103-the-biggest-threat-to-medicare-youve-never -even-heard-of/.

Kearney, John R. "Social Security and the 'D' in OASDI: The History of a Federal Program Insuring Earners against Disability." *Social Security Bulletin* 66, no. 3 (2006): 1–27. https://www.ssa.gov/policy/docs/ssb/v66n3/v66n3p1 .html.

Kenney, Erica L., Jessica L. Barrett, Sara N. Bleich, Zachary J. Ward, Angie L. Cradock, and Steven L. Gortmaker. "Impact of the Healthy, Hunger-Free Kids Act on Obesity Trends." *Health Affairs* 39, no. 7 (2020). https://doi.org/10 .1377/hlthaff.2020.00133.

Lagisetty, Pooja, Laura Flamm, Summer Rak, Jessica Landgraf, Michele Heisler, and Jane Forman. "A Multi-stakeholder Evaluation of the Baltimore City Virtual Supermarket Program." *BMC Public Health* 17, no. 1 (2017): 837. https://doi.org/10.1186/s12889-017-4864-9.

Laurence, Bethany K. "Are Social Security Benefits Taxed?" NOLO. Updated January 13, 2022. https://www.nolo.com/legal-encyclopedia/are-social -security-disability-benefits-taxed.html.

Lebergott, Stanley. "Labor Force and Employment, 1800–1960." In *Output, Employment, and Productivity in the United States after 1800*, ed. Dorothy S. Brady, 117–204. NBER, 1996. https://www.nber.org/system/files/chapters /c1567/c1567.pdf.

Long, Huey. "Share Our Wealth." Huey Long: The Man, His Mission, and Legacy. Accessed April 12, 2019. https://www.hueylong.com/programs/share -our-wealth.php.

McLaughlin, Jim. "Students Strike Against New Federal School Lunch Rules." *Milwaukee Journal Sentinel*. September 17, 2012. https://archive.jsonline.com /news/education/students-strike-against-new-federal-school-lunch-rules -t96t7sp-170124676.html/.

MORE Health Education Act, H.R. 987, 116th Cong. (2021). https://www .govinfo.gov/content/pkg/BILLS-116hr987ih/pdf/BILLS-116hr987ih.pdf.

O'Connell, Ann. "How to Delay an Eviction in Alabama." NOLO. Accessed April 17, 2022. https://www.nolo.com/legal-encyclopedia/how-to-delay-an -eviction-in-alabama.html.

Office of Family Assistance. "What We Do." U.S. Department of Health and Human Services. Last updated February 9, 2021. https://www.acf.hhs.gov/ofa /about/what-we-do.

Ortaliza, Jared, Giorlando Ramirez, Venkatish Satheeskumar, and Krutika Amin. "How Does U.S. Life Expectancy Compare to Other Countries?" KFF Health

System Tracker. Updated September 28, 2021. https://www.healthsystemtracker
.org/chart-collection/u-s-life-expectancy-compare-countries/.

Pradhan, Rachana. "Why Millions on Medicaid Are at Risk of Losing Coverage in the Months Ahead." *NPR*. February 14, 2022. https://www.npr.org/sections /health-shots/2022/02/14/1080295015/why-millions-on-medicaid-are-at-risk -of-losing-coverage-in-the-months-ahead.

Potter, Wendell. "Medicare Advantage—or DISAdvantage?" *Healthinsurance .org*. April 18, 2013. https://www.healthinsurance.org/blog/medicare -advantage-or-disadvantage/.

Recognizing the duty of the Federal Government to create a Green New Deal, H.Res. 109, 116th Con. (2019). https://www.congress.gov/bill/116th-congress /house-resolution/109/text.

Rose, Patti. "Medicare and Medicaid." In *Health Disparities, Diversity and Inclusion Context, Controversies, and Solutions*, 1st ed. (Burlington, MA: Jones and Bartlett Learning, 2018), 72–73.

Rudowitz, Robin, Rachel Garfield, and Elizabeth Hinton. "10 Things to Know about Medicaid: Setting the Facts Straight." Kaiser Family Foundation. March 6, 2019. https://www.kff.org/medicaid/issue-brief/10-things-to-know -about-medicaid-setting-the-facts-straight/.

Sandefur, Rebecca L. "Accessing Justice in the Contemporary USA: Findings from the Community Needs and Services Survey." American Bar Foundation (University of Illinois at Urbana-Champaign). Last updated August 8, 2014. https://www.americanbarfoundation.org/uploads/cms/documents/sandefur _accessing_justice_in_the_contemporary_usa._aug._2014.pdf.

Schott, Liz. "Why TANF Is Not a Model for Other Safety Net Programs." Center on Budget and Policy Priorities. Updated June 6, 2016. https://www .cbpp.org/research/family-income-support/why-tanf-is-not-a-model-for-other -safety-net-programs.

Shah, Rajiv. "A Strong Earned Income Tax Credit Will Help Americans Weather an Era of Crisis." *Fortune*. September 16, 2021. https://fortune.com/2021/09 /16/earned-income-tax-credit-benefits-eitc-expansion/.

Spalding, Matthew. "Why the U.S. Has a Culture of Dependency." *CNN*. September 21, 2012. https://www.cnn.com/2012/09/21/opinion/spalding -welfare-state-dependency/index.html.

State Budget and Tax. "Policy Basics: State Earned Income Tax Credits." Center on Budget and Policy Priorities. Last updated October 13, 2021. https://www .cbpp.org/research/state-budget-and-tax/state-earned-income-tax-credits.

Stein Berman, Rachel, Milani R. Patel, Peter F. Belamarich, and Rachel S. Gross. "Screening for Poverty and Poverty-Related Social Determinants of Health." *Pediatrics in Review* 39, no. 5 (2018): 235–46. https://doi.org/10.1542/pir .2017-0123.

Tobin-Tyler, Elizabeth, and Joel B. Teitelbaum. *Essentials of Health Justice: A Primer*. 1st ed. Burlington, MA: Jones and Bartlett Learning, 2019.

Wallace, Edward V. "Health Disparities: Using Policies to Rethink Our Strategies for Eliminating the Impact of Food Deserts by Focusing on Unhealthy Dietary Patterns." *Journal of Public Affairs* 19, no. 3 (2019). https://doi.org/10.1002/pa.1875.

Winters, Mike. "Rising Inflation Has Made It More Expensive to Eat at Home." *CNBC News.* April 12, 2022. https://www.cnbc.com/2022/04/12/how-much-grocery-prices-increased-as-inflation-reaches-41-year-high.html.

Xavier University. "Pharmacy Hosts 12th Annual Health Disparities Conference." Updated April 8, 2019. https://www.xula.edu/news/2019/04/pharmacy-hosts-12th-annual-health-disparities-conference.html.

SEVEN

Urban Health

Where We Go from Here, and What We Should Do

HEALTH DISPARITIES in urban neighborhoods are a widespread, complex issue where people of color living in poverty are systematically oppressed by those at the top of the social, economic, and political ladder. However, my experience of living in one of the poorest housing projects in all of New York City and of interviewing families from low-income neighborhoods across the country has impressed upon me that individuals are resilient. Just like health disparities, resilience can be passed on from one generation to the next, having a positive impact on the lives of people who live in low-income urban neighborhoods.

For generations, African Americans have had to shoulder the pain of their ancestors and develop resilience within themselves and their children; if not, Black people would no longer be in existence.[1] To be Black in America means you must have thick skin. This has aided Black people and protected us from being psychologically damaged in so many ways. Resilience will never fully stop the bleeding from the years of trauma, but it will reinforce the stitching to slow it down so that future trauma is less painful. That is why I believe that African Americans can live healthier lives no matter where they come from and the conditions in their neighborhood.

It is never easy to eliminate health disparities in low-income urban neighborhoods, and the changing and implementation of policies never seems to happen quick enough for those who struggle the most. Oftentimes we see that policy makers are unaware that a problem exists or misunderstand the nature of the problem, making it difficult to direct resources to people in need. Making innovative policy changes that yield improvements in the health of people who reside in low-income urban neighborhoods is possible, if we do not take a one-size-fits-all approach. One important course of action we must pursue is to change how the government views low-income urban neighborhoods. If policy makers believe that people who reside in low-income urban neighborhoods are lazy, thuggish, unmotivated criminals, just sitting at home and waiting for a welfare check to be hand-delivered to them, then this viewpoint ultimately determines what action is or is not taken in these particular neighborhoods.

There is a lot more we can and should do to eliminate health disparities in low-income urban neighborhoods, e.g., raising public awareness of racial and ethnic health disparities, assessing political candidates' decisions on addressing health disparities, and ensuring that Democratic and Republican presidential nominees make health disparities a priority issue and have a broad plan to address the social determinants of health. We can make sure that people who live in low-income urban neighborhoods get better access to education and training, which makes them more likely to find jobs that provide better benefits such as health insurance, paid leave, and retirement. Income has a major effect on health, and families with more education tend to earn more money, can more easily purchase healthier foods, have more time to exercise, and can more easily pay for health services and transportation.[2] When I interviewed Sabrina Whittredge, she explained to me how she wishes she had encouraged her family members, especially her niece Phoebe, to pursue careers in science, technology, engineering, and mathematics (colloquially known as STEM):

> I wish I knew what I know now back then. I would have pushed my niece Phoebe harder to excel in math and technology. . . . If you told me 20 years ago that we would be using cell phones and computers to talk to one another in real time, where I could see your face and

you could see mine as we are speaking to one another, I would have said you were crazy, but look at us now. It's remarkable what a person can do with a good education. . . . Don't get me wrong, I'm happy and proud that my niece has two college degrees and can do more with her education than what I could ever do with my high school education. What I'm saying is that if she had majored in science or engineering or something like that . . . when it comes to her finding a job, she would be able to name her own price.

Having a high-quality education is a major reason why parents who have attended college themselves are pushing their children to major in STEM disciplines. They are well aware that individuals with a low-quality education often have lower wages and are more vulnerable during hard times, which can lead to poor nutrition choices, discriminatory housing, unmet medical needs, and job insecurity.

People who live in low-income neighborhoods are often marginalized and experience more factors that contribute to poor health, such as less access to supermarkets, an oversupply of fast-food restaurants, a shortage of primary physicians, higher crime rates, higher levels of pollution and toxins, and less political influence to advocate for community needs. The result is a cycle of disadvantage.

How can we eliminate health disparities? Through policy changes. Yet, many people do not understand what laws and policies are or how they work.

Policy Matters More Now Than Ever Before

Laws and policies are blunt, brutal instruments that do not just make things disappear by magic, but through a real-world process of enforcement. No matter how serious or silly a public policy may be, it will affect people's lives and health. Every word written in a policy is there for a reason. Many people have been conditioned to be satisfied with "Don't worry—we put that in every document." If you do not understand the language or the wording that is put in a policy, you need to make sure that it gets explained to your satisfaction or have the person use different words in that policy or document so that you can fully understand it. This may be a matter of life or death when it comes to your health.[3] When you sign a document or agree to a health policy, always remember that you are now relying on the language of that document or policy that you signed or agreed with to protect your legal rights.

Historically some people have been excluded from accessing basic needs due to unfair policies that create barriers to health in low-income urban neighborhoods. At the end of slavery came Jim Crow laws (which formed a rigid pattern of racial segregation) and an unfair economic system that left little room for ambition and hope, perpetrating unequal education, humiliation, and brutalization. In the South, discriminatory policies allowed whites to be served in restaurants but not Blacks, resulting in sit-in demonstrations at restaurant establishments.[4] At the conclusion of the *Brown v. Board of Education* trial, the National Guard had to be ordered to protect Black students who had been discriminated against from an angry mob of white protesters who prevented them from entering a school in Arkansas on the first day of classes.[5] Mexican American farm workers in California went on strike in 1962, a movement known as La Causa, because they were being discriminated against and sought better health benefits, wage, and working conditions.[6] We know that in Dallas County, Alabama, during the Selma to Montgomery marches, a group of peaceful protesters were attacked by local law enforcement to prevent Black voters from registering, an event known as "Bloody Sunday."[7] The way I see it, it does not matter what type of racism people experience, whether it is systemic or institutional; the reality is that racist and discriminatory laws and policies over time lead to a number of health-related problems, such as heart disease, high blood pressure, chronic stress, and death, just to name a few.

Ultimately, it would be difficult to have substandard housing, poor nutrition, toxic environments, and health care gaps of every kind if people who were the most impacted were at the table when it came to designing, implementing, and enforcing policies. I realized a few years ago how valuable it was to be a part of the political process. I remember listening to Dr. Ibram X. Kendi speak at the 42nd National Council for Black Studies Conference. He said, "If you do not engage in politics, then you are a slave." At that moment, I did not understand what he meant. But after listening to him explain his point, it dawned upon me what he was actually trying to get across to the audience.[8] He was saying that if people do not engage in politics, then they are allowing others to dictate their lives and tell them how to live in society, just as the slave master dictates the life of their slaves and tells them how they should live on the slave master's plantation. This changed my life. My fight for health equity and justice became the focus of my work and I learned that if I really wanted to advance health equity, then I needed to address power and oppression.

Laws and Policies: Helping People Living in Low-Income Urban Neighborhoods to Obtain Legal Services

For individuals and families who live in low-income urban neighborhoods, one way to address power and oppression is to find a network of publicly funded legal aid agencies. Oftentimes these agencies will provide legal services for free or nearly free of charge. Legal aid agencies do not handle cases that involve the criminal court, only the civil court. Each legal aid office has its own rules and qualifications for its services. Therefore, it is very important to research the legal aid agencies in your area to find out who can help you with your legal problem. Some legal aid offices get funding from the government, so that may limit the type of cases the agency can accept. All legal aid lawyers have the same qualifications as other lawyers, which means that all legal information is confidential and will not be shared with anyone outside of the legal aid agency.

Equally important, but hardly ever used, are local bar associations. Individuals and families living in poverty can call their local bar association and ask to speak with the Lawyer Referral Directory. In many cases, families will be connected with a licensed private lawyer who has experience with the type of legal problems they are experiencing and may help for a reduced fee. Everyone should read the agreement carefully before hiring the lawyer to begin their case. Many times there is no fee, but the lawyer will get paid if they win their case. Individuals and families experiencing poverty can also ask their local bar association if they offer free services such as a pro bono project (also known as a volunteer lawyer project), a free legal workshop, or a self-help clinic.

Law schools are another means of helping individuals and families with lower incomes obtain legal services. Law schools have free legal clinics, at which law students provide free legal help to their clients but are always supervised by a law professor. If we contend that people living in low-income urban neighborhoods are constantly getting the short end of the stick when it comes to civil matters, then it is only right to connect them with future lawyers who are coming out of law school trained in advocating for social justice. If we truly realize how much poverty impacts the health of people in low-income urban neighborhoods, then exposing law students to real-world clients with lower incomes is a good way for individuals and families to have access to free legal aid and an opportunity for fundamental change through class action lawsuits.[9]

Affordable Care Act: One Step Forward, Two Steps Back

Before the Affordable Care Act came into existence, insurance companies were not obligated to provide health insurance to anyone who had a preexisting health condition. In March 2010, the Affordable Care Act was signed into law by former President Barack Obama to prevent insurance companies from excluding people with preexisting conditions. It has been proven that the Affordable Care Act has had a positive impact on the lives of many Americans, especially those experiencing poverty. A national study by the National Health Interview Survey found that between 2013 and 2014, after many states implemented the Affordable Care Act, the uninsured rates for Black and Hispanic adults decreased tremendously, even more than the rates for white adults.[10] For many of these states, the Affordable Care Act has eliminated a number of racial disparities among individuals living in poverty.

Donald Trump's administration repealed parts of the Affordable Care Act but did not replace it with an alternative plan. When the Trump administration repealed the Affordable Care Act during the first year of his term in office, 18 million people were left without health insurance.

Black Women and Giving Birth: Mental Health, Chronic Stress, Resistance, and Their Health Outcomes

With all the talk around health disparities, we might ask how it is that in every low-income urban neighborhood in the United States, people feel that good health is nearly impossible to achieve. As a researcher, I argue that a large part of the problem is racism and how it affects low-income urban neighborhoods. To fully comprehend the issue, we need to look at what Black women face in giving birth when they live in low-income urban neighborhoods.

As mothers, Black women play a key role in the sustainable development and quality of life in the Black family, whether they are single or partnered. However, when we look at the health outcomes of Black women during pregnancy, we see that they have worse pregnancy outcomes than those of white women. Black women are three times more likely to miscarry or experience stillbirth than white women, and four times more likely to lose their own lives during childbirth compared to white women.[11]

Unfortunately, many health professionals are unaware or seem to forget the profound historical weight of racism and sexism that Black women carry. So let's revisit why Black women experience miscarriages and stillbirths. One of the reasons why this happens is chronic stress. When health professionals hear this, they are quick to come up with some stress management techniques that tend to work for the general population, but not necessarily Black women. These techniques normally include things like yoga, aromatherapy, pet therapy, massages, and hot baths.

When a Black woman enters a doctor's office for mental health counseling, she is not entering by herself. She is coming into that office with the weight of misogyny, sexism, and racism on her shoulders that not only she had to endure, but the misogyny, sexism, and racism that her mother, grandmother, and even great-grandmother had to experience. So what does this look like in respect to Black women? In modern-day society, it looks like trauma, disassociation, hopelessness, depression, and anxiety, which contribute to stress, which in turn are related to poor pregnancy outcomes.

Now, when we look at the social determinants of health as they apply to neighborhoods, we see that there are some clear differences between wealthy neighborhoods and impoverished neighborhoods. Wealthy neighborhoods often have more human and social capital, which include better schools with more qualified teachers, more access to healthier foods, green spaces, and parks for recreation. People tend to have a better connection with their neighbors in terms of social norms, culture, and overall positivity. They also tend to have more married families.[12] A evidence-based study revealed that marriages improve certain mental health outcomes, reduce the use of some high-cost services (such as nursing homes), and increase the likelihood of having health insurance.[13] On the other hand, in many low-income neighborhoods, we often see people having a minimum standard of living. For example, children in low-income neighborhoods often attend low-performing schools, there are no or very few Black-owned businesses, there is gun violence in the streets, and there are no clean or safe places to play.[14] All of this can prevent people who experience poverty from participating in mainstream society.

Historical Timeline of African Americans: We Are No Longer the Same People

Ever since African Americans were enslaved and brought to the United States, they have been on the defensive and find it very difficult to trust white people. African Americans that were enslaved had their language, culture, and identity taken from them by whites. So when we look at health, particularly mental health, understanding social and cultural identity is a valuable part of the whole. African Americans in this country have had to rebuild their identities to the standards of white culture. They have had to ask themselves: how much education should I pursue? What religion should I practice? What foods should I eat? What language should I speak? All of these standards that have been forced upon Blacks are European standards, not standards of African descent. As an African American, I have been made into a person that is not myself. My DNA tells me that I am a totally different person, not the individual that my ancestors taught me to be in life.

In 1865, which marked the end of the Civil War, Black people were considered to be free. But then the Black codes were enforced, which forced Blacks to work as cheap labor on farms.[15] This was in reality a form of slavery, especially if Blacks owed a debt to that farm owner. This put Black people on the defensive, not knowing who to trust. Also occurring during this time was the rise of the Ku Klux Klan, which terrorized African Americans with brutal force and cultivated an atmosphere of fear.[16] Once again, this put African Americans on the defensive of not being able to trust whites.

During early Reconstruction, from 1865 to 1877, the Union army remained in the South to protect Blacks and their land so they could be free and safe. Eventually the Union army was pulled out, and many whites took land back from free African Americans and placed them back into slavery.[17] This led to mistrust and African Americans finding themselves on the defensive once again.

From 1877 to 1928, there were convict leasing laws where a white person could accuse a Black person of a crime that they did not commit and that Black individual would be convicted and sent to a work camp, which was essentially a plantation for slavery.[18] Around the same time period (from 1877 to the 1950s), the Jim Crow laws were in effect.[19] The Jim Crow laws separated whites from Blacks and prevented them from being in contact with any person of color (at parks, theatres, restaurants, and so on) to ensure that they were not treated equally.

The 1950s and 1960s saw the rise of the civil rights movement.[20] In the 1970s, the FBI infiltrated Black organizations, such as the Black Panther Party, and killed their leaders.[21] During the 1980s, crack was introduced to inner cities and low-income neighborhoods, destroying the Black community.[22]

Today's challenges include the prison industrial system and gentrification in urban areas, where Black people experiencing poverty are being displaced from their own neighborhoods.[23] Throughout all of this, every low-income urban neighborhood is trying to rebound from being on the defensive because of what has historically happened to individuals and their families as a result of racism. The idea of being on the defensive and not trusting others is what kept African Americans alive for so many years. The explanation of this historical timeline is crucial because by the time you reach the end of the timeline, you realize that people of African descent are no longer the same people that they were before.

Latinos and Resistance: Protecting Each Other's Mental Health through Community

The hearts, minds, and souls of Hispanics have also been attacked by whites in our society. Many Puerto Ricans in particular feel the pressure of having to choose between being Latino or American and having to respond with resilience when they are constantly faced with the struggle of being one or the other. Many people are not aware that Puerto Ricans are US citizens or that Puerto Rico is a part of the United States. Rosa Santoya talks about how she is questioned and discriminated against all the time in the United States. She states,

> I still get asked, "How did you get your work permit?" or "Can you show me a second form of ID (her passport) along with your driver's license?" The microaggressions of where people ask you to prove your status more often than they would ask someone else is daunting on Puerto Ricans because it's a reminder that white Americans don't often show regard to Latinos as human beings or Americans.

For Latinos who live in urban areas in the United States, this is shocking because when Puerto Ricans are back home in Puerto Rico, they are proud of and love the relationship between Puerto Rico and the United States.[24]

When talking to Rosa, she spoke about living in Puerto Rico and in the United States. "One of the beautiful things about going home to Puerto Rico is that I appreciate it because this is who I am. But living in the United States, I have gained a different perspective because not everyone wants to know what it's like being a Puerto Rican." One of the biggest misconceptions about resilience is that it is an individual act, and that a single person bounces back from misfortune. The reality is that resilience derives not just from your own inner strength, but also from the words and actions of people who care about you.[25]

For many Puerto Ricans, when they are met with discrimination and adversity, they rely on the bonds and relationships from other people who make up their world.[26] They show their resilience by being in constant connection with their family, friends, and country.[27] Oftentimes Puerto Ricans are encouraged by other Puerto Ricans to keep an open mind, have a positive attitude, and always challenge those in power despite the consequences.

Challenging Those in Power

For low-income urban neighborhoods to achieve good health, people must challenge the system. Having those in power appreciate the value of African Americans and other marginalized communities is crucial to the success of Blacks and other vulnerable populations. This is not something new. Rosa Parks challenged the system and refused to give up her seat on a bus for a white passenger and started the Montgomery bus boycott, led by Dr. Martin Luther King Jr. Thirteen months later, the city of Montgomery, Alabama, realized the value and economic power that the Black community contributed to the local bus company. They came up with a compromise that ended the bus boycott, stating that Blacks could sit wherever they wanted on the bus.[28]

Four Black students from North Carolina A&T State University challenged the system by starting a nonviolent sit-in at a segregated lunch counter at F.W. Woolworth's in Greensboro, North Carolina. For months, these students were denied service and not allowed to sit at the lunch counter. Sitting at the counter when this was prohibited by law was the students' way of stating that they refused to be ignored and that they had value, and were worthy of sitting at the same lunch counter as their white counterparts and being served a meal. Six months after the sit-ins, the original protestors were served lunch at the same Woolworth's lunch counter where they were first denied.[29]

On March 7, 1965, a day known as "Bloody Sunday," Blacks marched from Selma to Montgomery, Alabama, to challenge the system in support of voting rights, only to be stopped on the Edmund Pettus Bridge by police, where they were attacked with billy clubs, tear gas, and whips. Despite this horrific incident, Blacks still decided to show the world—on national television—their strength, perseverance, and dignity. The display of their tenacity and worth was not just for the world to see, but for their children and grandchildren to see and experience so they may have the right to vote. As a direct consequence of this event, the United States passed the Voting Rights Act of 1965, guaranteeing every American 21 years of age and older the right to register and vote regardless of their religion, gender, sexual orientation, socioeconomic status, race, or ethnicity.[30]

Inner-City Highways: Displacing and Destroying Neighborhoods

Sadly, some people do not feel as though racism is a problem that often can be detrimental to someone's health. A national poll found that 36% of Americans said that racism exists, but it is not a major problem in society. In that same poll, 47% of Americans said that they benefit from or enjoy advantages in society that other racial and ethnic groups do not have.[31] Health disparities are dictated by a number of social determinants of health, such as race, class, and geographical location. As a first step, policy makers, community leaders, scholars, educators, and parents of the world must have conversations about race and racism with young children. For example, children need to understand that urban freeways were systematically built in certain neighborhoods. The government placed freeways in almost every low-income neighborhood that was largely populated by people of color.[32]

Ultimately these highways destroyed and displaced entire neighborhoods, resulting in the abandonment of businesses, high crime levels, pollution, and economic downfall, all of which were fueled by racism.[33] Placing freeways through inner-cities do not make low-income neighborhoods look attractive. The only problem that gets solved from having freeways slice through an inner-city neighborhood is to move cars from point A to point B. Since it appears federal and state transportation planners are not interested in the health and well-being of people who experience poverty, then it will be up to activists who care about people who live in poverty to act on their behalf.

Community Initiatives That Are Making Real-World Changes

A number of successful community initiatives are driving long-lasting real-world change. In California's Central Valley, a low-income community partnered up with a grassroots organization that empowered the community's residents with the knowledge and skills to understand policies and city plans. This has led to on-the-ground changes which have enhanced health and equity in that community.[34] Teaching people in low-income urban neighborhoods how to conduct research and have clear ideas on how to improve health also works. Critical research, advocacy, leadership, and policy-making skills are also key ingredients for standing up for change. Many of my colleagues across the world are focused on health equity in low-income neighborhoods. As a scholar and activist, I have participated in a number of training sessions, workshops, and conferences to educate people from underserved neighborhoods and provide them with the tools to advocate for change. Having a long, healthy life—no matter your race, gender, economic status, or place of residence—starts with having a real conversation about creating opportunities.

K–12 Education: Targeting Health Disparities and Health Equity

For each individual and family who is fighting for health equity for their neighborhood, there seems to be a law or policy that hinders health equity and public health policy efforts. So what can we do to help low-income urban neighborhoods overcome health disparities? A creative solution is to do what we did in the early 1990s with education.

This is not a new idea, but it seems to have had an impact. When I graduated from college, many of my undergraduate friends that majored in early and secondary education were approached by schools from inner cities and given a unique opportunity. The proposal was that upon completion of their undergraduate degree, they would teach in a low-income school district and, for their services, the state would pay for them to complete their master's degree in education within five years. This agreement worked for both sides because cities such as New York City were able to recruit some of the top teachers in the state and help close the education gap, and students were able to work in their profession straight out of college and have their graduate education paid for in full, free of charge.

This same concept can be applied to people in the health professions or medical field. Students who have an interest in health disparities and health equity could be targeted in high school and tracked until they enter into college. After students enter into college and take a number of courses in health disparities and health equity, the students could be offered a job upon graduation for a non-profit organization, or a city or state health department that focuses on eliminating health disparities in low-income urban neighborhoods for a minimum of five years. In exchange for the five-year term, students could have their graduate education paid for in full and or have their undergraduate loans forgiven.

Recognizing Unconscious Bias and Stereotypes

For students majoring in law, health care, health policy, political science, public health law, social work, or legal epidemiology, an educational approach to teaching these students the importance of recognizing, managing, and monitoring their own implicit biases is essential for reducing health disparities. For example, legal epidemiology looks at the impact of law and legal practices on health and challenges the legal decisions made by non-lawyers in the health system.[35] A course of study that examines the cultural tensions between law and health is a great way for students to confront their own prejudices. As mentioned earlier in this chapter, the effects of discrimination, stereotyping, and racism—both conscious and subconscious—can have deeply negative impacts and influence the health of people who live in low-income urban neighborhoods. A recent study showed that physicians were more likely to view urban Blacks as non-active participants in a physician-patient relationship because in their view, the patients did not communicate effectively. In the same study, urban Blacks were more likely than whites to report that during their last physician's visit, the physician did not discuss test or examination findings with them at all.[36]

Another study was conducted on race in the labor market, using identical resumes that were randomly sent out to several corporations in Boston and Chicago who were looking to hire employees. One resume was labeled with a white-sounding name, "Emily," while the other resume—with the exact same credentials, such as levels of education and years of experience—was labeled with an African American name, "Lakisha." The study revealed that white-sounding names received 50% more callbacks or emails for interviews across all occupations compared to Black-sounding names.[37] We still live in a society where unconscious bias and unequal treatment by race appears to be prominent in the workforce. This ultimately impacts economic stability in low-income urban neighborhoods populated by people of color, which in return influences a person's health.

Having small conversations about biases is not getting the job done in terms of educating people about the impact of implicit bias. Some researchers are making the argument that education about implicit bias needs to focus around a number of key elements, such as, but not limited to:[38]

1. Having a basic understanding of other people's cultures;
2. Recognizing situations that magnify bias and stereotypes;
3. Avoiding stereotyping individuals;
4. Practicing and working toward understanding unconscious bias;
5. Believing in the principle that all people are equal and deserve equal opportunities;
6. Recognizing how implicit bias can influence others, even when one does not think that it does.

Even though not much is known about whether health professionals and law makers are practicing self-reflection and recognizing how implicit bias impacts health, I believe that the issue needs to be in the forefront of our future policy and a priority for our policy makers if we plan on closing the ever-increasing health disparities in low-income urban communities.

Call for an Increase in Student Diversity in Medical Schools

Policy changes can also increase student diversity in medical schools and health professions. Increasing faculty, staff, and student diversity continues to be a problem. There are many individuals experiencing poverty who live in low-income neighborhoods and have the talent, work ethic, and intellectual capacity to become physicians, give back to their neighborhoods, and close the disparities gap, but they will most likely never be given this opportunity unless we make changes to our policies in our academic institutions. A few years ago, the Liaison Committee on Medical Education put out a policy stating that in order for medical schools to maintain their accreditation, they had to change their standard as it relates to the academic and learning environment in which they serve.[39] The policy read as follows: "An institution that sponsors a medical education program must have effective policies and practices in place, and engage in ongoing, systematic, and focused recruitment and retention activities, to achieve mission-appropriate diversity outcomes among its students, faculty, administrative staff and members of its academic community."

To my knowledge, based on a review of the literature, medical education programs are one of the few health professions that include diversity as part of the criteria for accreditation for a medical program.[40] With this bold move, we should be optimistic about seeing more people from low-income urban neighborhoods attending medical school in the future.

Reinvesting in Health: Providing Low-Income Neighborhoods with Funding and Resources

Low-income urban neighborhoods are more than capable of solving problems in their own communities, if given the resources and funding. We should not just throw money at a particular problem, but rather align money with real, measurable goals and opportunities.

When I am in New York City, visiting the Hughes family, I see a number of boarded-up apartment buildings that landlords have deemed undesirable but are willing to sell. Dave Hughes mentioned this in a conversation that we had:

> Why won't the city do something with these buildings instead of letting them just go to waste? We are New Yorkers—people in other cities look to us for answers. I can't believe these buildings are not being used for some type of good for the community . . . like low-income housing or a health clinic or something like that. I pass by these abandoned buildings every day and all I can do is shake my head in disgust.

Non-traditional settings can help reduce health disparities in low-income urban neighborhoods. Shopping malls and strip malls across the country are closing down in increasing numbers because of large retail distributors such as Amazon.[41] Sabrina stated, "We have a strip mall two blocks from my house. The only store that is worth going in and buying anything is Family Dollar, and they get robbed so much, they are about to close down. Those other stores in that strip mall are never in business. It seems like every six months there is a leasing sign in one of the windows."

The decline of shopping malls and strip malls is happening at a time when health care needs are growing and medical care is becoming more community-based.[42] In low-income areas, underutilized shopping malls and strip malls could be transformed into medical malls, which could increase access to health care and stimulate the local economy in disadvantaged neighborhoods.

Cultural and Linguistic Competence

We must continue to recognize the importance of cultural and linguistic competence and its significant role in health care. Ferdinand and Mercedes Ruiz have shared with me that it is easy to discuss cultural and linguistic competence but much more difficult to implement it, especially when we all view the world differently and many of us seek health care in an environment where our predominant language is not spoken. If we ever plan on reducing health disparities in low-income urban neighborhoods, then a key strategy for policy makers and health service organizations is to develop and implement a robust cultural and linguistic competency plan.

The first step in developing this plan is to do away with the one-size-fits-all approach and replace it with a diversity and inclusion system. Many scholars view cultural competence and diversity as a single cohesive unit. A cultural competency plan basically says that we can eliminate health disparities if we implement policies that broaden our understanding of cultural differences and encourage us to work with one another in cross-cultural spaces.[43] In addition, if you have a cultural competency plan, then you must also have a linguistic competency plan. Linguistic competency is a key component of culture competency, as language is a major part of culture. It is the responsibility of those who are in health services and public health to meet the needs of those individuals who are most affected at every level.[44]

If the predictions are correct that by the year 2050, African Americans and Hispanics will be the majority while whites will be considered the minority in the United States, then this means that if we do not address health disparities today, the majority of Americans will suffer from inadequate health care and die sooner than their white counterparts.[45] Amid the changing demographics of society, the need to include a cultural and linguistic competency plan is essential to eliminating health disparities and improving the health outcomes of low-income urban neighborhoods.

Equitable Development Policy: A Way for Gentrification to Work for the Poor

City decision makers, planners, and developers must think about how gentrification affects the heath of low-income urban neighborhoods. Gentrification has always had a strong racial component, wherein lower-income African American residents and other residents of color are replaced with higher-income white residents. The reason why this residential segregation occurs is mainly due to tactics used by private and public institutions. The goal for many politicians, including mayors in cities across the country, is to attract middle-class and wealthy residents to their cities so they can revitalize the tax base for their communities and bring vibrancy to their neighborhoods and downtowns.[46] If city officials, developers, residents, and policy makers support equitable development policies, then stable economic neighborhoods can be created without the burden of displacement falling unfairly on residents who live in poverty and oftentimes have nowhere else to go.[47]

An equitable development policy will make gentrification work for low-income urban neighborhoods.[48] When the market value increases due to gentrification, city leaders can require developers to set aside affordable housing units for families with lower incomes.[49] By requiring developers to abide by this give-and-take, residents experiencing poverty can have affordable housing right next door to market-rate housing and not be forced to move out of their neighborhood. Another approach is to require landlords to pay relocation payments to residents with lower incomes.[50]

Health in All Policies

Health is considered one of our most precious resources. I encourage people in low-income urban neighborhoods to hold their local representatives accountable and make sure that health is included in all of the decisions that are being made about the people they serve in their congressional district. Having health in all policies is a step toward reducing health inequalities in urban neighborhoods. Policy changes, however small, matter.

Global Health Disparities: The United Kingdom's Approach to Addressing Health Inequalities

How are disparities in other countries similar to disparities seen in the United States? Currently, people are living longer in the United Kingdom, but oftentimes these individuals and their families are living in poorer health—and not just that, but many people who live in low-income urban areas will eventually have to deal with diseases and disability before they can collect their pensions and enjoy their retirement.[51] The United Kingdom and other countries are not much different than the United States.

Let's consider how the United Kingdom has tackled health inequalities. The United Kingdom was creating policies to address health inequalities long before many other countries, including the United States. The first attempt to address health inequalities dates back to 1977 with the creation of the Black Report,[52] which gave four explanations of why health inequalities existed in the United Kingdom. First was an artifact from previous generations. By using artifacts and telling stories about these objects, a person can interpret the day-to-day lives of individuals by the objects they once owned. For example, field experts can ask questions about health and well-being by investigating artifacts and how their owners might have used them. Through close examinations, field experts can then answer the question how people in the United Kingdom took care of their bodies.[53] Second is natural selection. Natural selection is the process by which living organisms adapt and change. This variation means some individuals have better traits suited for the environment in which they live.[54] Third is culture. Culture embraces a variety of beliefs, customs, and values.[55] The fourth and final factor is structural, which refers to macro-level conditions such as institutional policies that limit power and well-being to certain populations based on race or ethnicity.[56] However, in this report, there was no mention of how health care could play a role in reducing health inequalities.

The Conservative government, because of political hostility toward the issue, rejected the Black Report. In 1998, under a new government, the United Kingdom welcomed the Acheson Report to address health inequalities; this was an offshoot of the original Black Report. Unlike the Black Report, the Acheson Report addressed the social determinants of health in the UK. In fact, the Acheson Report examines specific areas of the social determinants of health, such as poverty, education, employment, housing, transportation, nutrition, ethnicity, gender, and health care.[57]

The United Kingdom's Sure Start program is an initiative which has effectively addressed health inequalities for children living in poverty.[58] In the beginning of the implementation of the Sure Start program, only children who lived in certain areas would have access to services; these services primarily consisted of early childhood education for families living in poverty.[59] The success of this program came with changing the pattern of existing services and putting an emphasis on preventative services for families. For example, the program provided families with child care and health care. The United Kingdom's Sure Start program also put a great amount of emphasis on helping poor families start careers. The reason for helping poor families to begin careers was to cut down on crime and unemployment and reduce the need for extra help from state benefits later on in life.[60] Giving poor families and their children a great start in life is a fundamental part of improving health and reducing health disparities.[61]

United Kingdom: Child Poverty Act 2010

The Child Poverty Act 2010 is another UK governmental initiative aimed at reducing the number of children living in poverty.[62] A study conducted by the Organization for Economic Co-operation and Development found that the United Kingdom has one of the highest rates of child poverty.[63] Since the UK government implemented the Child Poverty Act 2010 by raising welfare benefit levels and introducing new benefits that support low-paid workers and subsidize child care, a number of children have been "lifted out" of poverty.[64]

The increased focus on child poverty has led the UK government to consider social exclusion to be a core problem that needs to be addressed in the United Kingdom. The concept of social exclusion is when someone's resources (material, cultural, and social) are so limited that they are excluded from the minimum acceptable way of life in the areas in which they live.[65] This differs from the United States' federal poverty guidelines, used to measure poverty, which are produced by the Department of Health and Human Services.[66] In the US, poverty guidelines simply use the number of people in a family unit to determine poverty.

These guidelines are updated each year based on annual changes to the consumer price index and differ based on where people actually live.[67] For example, poverty in Manhattan, New York, will not be the same as poverty in Jackson, Mississippi.

With all the success that has been achieved with the implementation of the Child Poverty Act 2010, it should be noted that in 1999, then prime minister Tony Blair made the announcement that they would have child poverty eliminated by 2020. However, he was not the one who led the charge on child poverty, which has made significant progress. Public concern about children's deaths—and later about families' economic hardship in general—did it.[68]

Tobacco: The Fairness Doctrine and the Start of the Anti-smoking Movement

In the early 1950s, when British researchers found that there was an association between lung cancer and smoking, many American anti-smoking activists used this knowledge as an opportunity to go after the big tobacco companies in the United States.[69] In fact, anti-tobacco activists used a policy called the fairness doctrine, introduced in 1949, to start an anti-smoking movement. This legal doctrine required television broadcasters to present controversial topics to the public in an honest, balanced, and impartial way.[70]

Politicians and legislators were not responsible for this anti-tobacco movement. It was the American people's concern about health inequalities—and later about eliminating health disparities in lung cancer—that jump-started the tough policies that we have seen over the years on advertising regulations. Unfortunately, the Supreme Court abolished the fairness doctrine in 1987 on the grounds that it infringed on a person's right to freedom of speech, which is protected by and preserved in the First Amendment of the Constitution.[71] Since the 1990s, new anti-smoking activist groups have joined the fight against Big Tobacco.[72] Quite a few tactics were used to gain support for the movement. For example, activists called for boycotts of companies who were affiliated with tobacco companies, especially those who advertised toward children. Other anti-smoking campaigns consist of smoke-damaged, diseased body parts in an attempt to scare off smokers.[73] Today, we owe a great deal of gratitude to the anti-smoking activists because without their perseverance and tenacity, we would not be as far along as we are when it comes to creating a smoke-free environment.

Building Healthy and Equitable Communities: Transforming Schools

Lack of education and awareness about health disparities seems to dominate the conversation in many communities of color experiencing poverty. This is true for many of the chronic diseases and other health problems that are seen in low-income communities. I believe educating ourselves about health disparities and the policies that help eliminate these disparities is essential. But to accomplish this, we need to think big and be unapologetic about our approach in achieving this goal. One way we can do that is to build healthy, equitable communities through transforming the school climate.

When it comes to changing health policies, schools are probably better positioned than any other institution. In the United States, education policy always starts at the federal level, but implementation and enforcement take place at the state and local level. Too many schools in low-income communities lack the resources and support necessary to address students' health. It is no surprise that schools with declining infrastructure have lower test scores, chronic cases of absenteeism, increased rates of anxiety and depression, lower morale, and poorer health conditions. To most effectively respond to this crisis, we need to change the funding policies that are deeply rooted in historical inequalities, like neighborhood segregation. This means leveling the playing field and making sure that the state prevents inequitable funding systems like attendance-based financing, which is a policy that reduces state aid to schools on the basis of student absences.

How realistic are my recommendations, and what will it take to patch up the wounds that have caused so many in low-income urban neighborhoods to suffer from inadequate health policies? We first need to increase the amount of awareness amongst the general population, student population, and some policy makers about the magnitude of inequalities in health that exist in low-income urban neighborhoods. If the general and student populations are unaware that disparities exist, then we will never motivate and mobilize ourselves to do anything about existing health inequities. Second, we need empathy from policy makers on a personal and political level. It is not enough to just be aware of the problem. An emotional connection is needed if we are going to make real progress. Society needs to believe that health inequalities in low-income urban neighborhoods are unacceptable. We need to tell the stories about health inequities to the American population, so there can be some compassion toward low-income urban neighborhoods.

Enough Is Enough: The Next Generation of Young Leaders and Scholars

I am confident that the tenacity of today's young leaders will lead to new laws and policies that will ensure that all communities, especially low-income urban neighborhoods, are healthy and equitable. In the aftermath of the 2018 shooting that took place in Parkland, Florida, many of the student survivors called on Congress to pass legislation on gun control.[74] Mass school walkouts took place in every time zone, with dozens of students, from elementary schools to colleges and universities across the United States, protesting against gun violence.[75]

We also witnessed a man by the name of George Floyd beg for his life, telling police officers "I can't breathe" and calling for his mama numerous times while a Minneapolis police officer had his knee on Mr. Floyd's neck for 9 minutes and 29 seconds. This sparked protests all over the country, in more than 600 places, in all 50 states and Washington, DC.[76] We even saw citizens of Asia, Europe, Africa, Canada, Mexico, and the Caribbean conduct peaceful protests while joining in solidarity with the United States against racism and police brutality.[77] For instance, in Kingston, Jamaica, a peaceful protest was held outside the US embassy, where hundreds of protestors wore black to demand justice for George Floyd and the many Jamaicans who were killed by law enforcement.[78]

Our young people are speaking out, and they have a true desire to make this world a much better place than the one our past generations have left for them. Our young people are saying that enough is enough. We have witnessed some of the largest protests in US history. People want to do what is right. This was not the case in years past. Even though many people marched alongside Dr. Martin Luther King Jr. and other civil rights leaders during the 1960s, a good portion of white people were still not in favor of seeing Blacks get their fair share of equity and justice in society. When progressive whites allowed Blacks to be served at food counters in restaurants and when they decided Blacks no longer had to sit in the back of the bus, they understood that they did not have anything to worry about because they were not giving up any real power.

The protests on behalf of George Floyd, Breonna Taylor, and others were not the same protests as those in past years. The modern-day protests kept growing, they kept changing, and they were different. People were paying attention to what was happening and they were taking action. A large number of white people protested in the name of Black Lives Matter. This had never been done before at this magnitude. In some cities, there were more whites protesting in the streets than Blacks. We had law enforcement officials marching alongside the protesters and some police officers going as far as to take a knee with the protestors to display solidarity against police brutality.

This type of behavior was unheard of during the civil rights era. In 1963, at Kelly Ingram Park in Birmingham, Alabama, a 17-year-old boy who was peacefully protesting was confronted by a police officer and pushed backward by the officer.[79] At the same time, a police dog lunged forward in an aggressive manner, attacking and biting the young nonviolent protester. The police later attempted to cover up the story by accusing the boy of antagonizing the dog, causing the dog to become aggressive.

During the civil rights era, you never saw a police officer speak out against another police officer for using a dog as a tool for intimidation and violence against Black people—or, better yet, see a police officer take a knee alongside peaceful protestors fighting for equality and against police brutality. Every step of progress for freedom in this country came with a struggle, and the way our young people are winning this battle is to make people in power feel uncomfortable.

Young protestors are also making an impact when it comes to big corporations and major league sports. Netflix was one of the first companies to put out a statement saying that they were committing themselves to true systemic change. They are doing this by highlighting powerful and complex narratives about the Black experience. When you log onto Netflix today, you will see an array of titles that tell stories about racial injustice and Blackness in America.[80] The NBA also decided to take action when young athletes from the Milwaukee Bucks decided not to play basketball on the same day they heard of Jacob Blake's death.[81] This sparked a chain of events throughout the NBA, as other teams also decided to sit out games. Not only did the players boycott a few basketball games to bring focus to the issue of racial

The Foot Soldier sculpture depicts a police officer and police-trained dog attacking a young nonviolent protestor at Kelly Ingram Park in Birmingham, Alabama. *Source:* Allen Creative / Steve Allen / Alamy Stock Photo.

injustice, they also influenced the owners of the teams to get involved. As a result of these athletes banding together, owners partnered with the players' association and opened their basketball arenas to the general public (particularly people in low-income urban neighborhoods) so they could act on their constitutional right to vote in a presidential election.[82] Many of our young people are demanding more from our government at the local, state, and federal level. The young people want to end institutional and systemic racism in our society—that is why we are seeing a movement for reforming policing and the passing of the George Floyd Justice in Policing Act.

Reforming Policing: The George Floyd Justice in Policing Act

Protesting creates pressure for policies to get passed. Countless young men and women are saying that enough is enough and want to reform police departments across the country by introducing the George Floyd Justice in Policing Act.[83] This policy is unique because it seeks transparency and accountability. It will make it easier to prosecute police officers and hold them accountable. No longer will cops be able to protect bad police officers with their code of silence. The policy lends itself to shattering the "blue wall of silence" by getting rid of bad cops when they perform illegal and wrongful behavior while on duty. Second, the policy will allow a task force from the Department of Justice to create a nationwide database of police officers' wrongdoings while on the job. This prevents police officers from transferring from one department to another without the community knowing about their past history. This will help address the issue of transparency between the police and the community.

You are probably asking yourself: so what makes the George Floyd Justice in Policing Act so special? This brings me to my final point, the most important one. What makes this proposed policy special is that the bill looks to remove qualified immunity. All police officers have qualified immunity, meaning they cannot be sued on certain claims if the act occurred during their work hours. This was intended to give police officers added protection on the basis that they would have to put themselves in harm's way to apprehend and subdue suspects. By passing the George Floyd Justice in Policing Act, there is a clear message being sent that no one is above the law, including police officers.

Many would argue that if we remove the added protection of qualified immunity for police officers, we will turn people away from wanting to enter the field of law enforcement. If that's true, what about other disciplines? Doctors have to worry about malpractice lawsuits, and so do lawyers, but this does not interfere with their personal calling to practice medicine or law.

While many young peaceful protestors want change in this country, and the current atmosphere gives us the impression that the George Floyd Justice in Policing Act is the best way moving forward for Americans to create positive change, the passing of the act is not a slam dunk, not by a long shot. We must remember that we are a democracy and a nation that consists of powerful police unions who are opposed to the passing of the George Floyd Justice in Policing Act. Many of our Congressmen and Congresswomen who work in Washington, DC, were voted into those positions to serve their constituents. When elections come around, those in Congress are going to need votes again. Will Democrats and Republicans work together in getting the George Floyd Justice in Policing Act passed, or will lawmakers block the bill from being signed?

"Defund the Police" Policy

Many people are fighting for policies that defund the police and demand more transparency between the police and the community. I often tell people that we should not be afraid of the term "defund," because we defund programs and departments all the time in our society. When it comes to education, we are constantly defunding art, theatre, and music programs and no one is protesting in the streets about how our children's education is being stolen from them, right before our eyes. But now we are using the phrase "defund the police," and people are up in arms. The term "defund the police" has been used on a widespread basis in political arenas to make the American people believe that certain political parties are interested in getting rid of police officers and having communities without police. This is not the purpose of defunding the police.

When we look at the number of 911 calls on a daily basis, we tend to see police responding to calls for people who are experiencing homelessness and/or episodes of mental illness. Many police officers are not trained to respond to violent acts of self-harm or recognize if someone has a mental health issue that affects their ability to communicate or identify social cues, or determine what is real.[84] For example, a man in Houston, Texas, put a TV in a cart at Walmart, and did not try to hide the fact as he walked right out of the store. When the sales clerk caught up with him, the man stated "I have received a satellite message from God to take this TV." In the past, law enforcement would have thrown this person in jail, focusing on the criminal component of the event and not the person.[85] Young activists and protestors are demanding that we implement policies where police departments use trained, community-based professionals, such as social workers and homeless outreach workers, to handle certain emergency situations, such as mental health crisis and substance abuse calls.[86] The data has shown that having unarmed service providers is a "better fit" in instances when responding to a call about someone wielding a weapon. In fact, the response team having a weapon only escalates the situation.[87] It is unfair to ask a police officer to do the job of a social worker or a crisis intervention worker, and it's also wrong to perpetuate the criminalization of homelessness and mental illness. This is the purpose of defunding the police and why activists and protestors are pushing for these policies. Young protestors are beginning to reimagine what communities might look like in the twenty-first century if we can shift the response to nonviolent 911 calls to crisis intervention workers instead of needing law enforcement to respond.

What will happen if city and state lawmakers do not take protestors and making defunding the police a top priority seriously? There are two possible outcomes. First, we will continue to have more of the same in our society, meaning we will continue to see a rise in the number of cases where people of color die at the hands of police officers due to racist and violent policing systems. Second, we will have more civil lawsuits brought against police departments.

In California, the police pulled over a woman and her fiancé for driving with expired registration tags. The couple was coming home from visiting their gynecologist at the doctor's office. The woman and her fiancé were ordered to get out of the car by the police. The woman stated to the police that she was pregnant and wanted to sit in the car. They refused. The police did not suspect her of any wrongdoing, and it was clearly visible to the police that she was pregnant. After ordering the woman to get out of the car again, the police yanked her out of the car and stomped on her stomach, leaving a shoeprint and causing her to have a miscarriage. The woman did not commit any crime, nor was she a suspect of any crime, and no criminal charges were filed against her. There is currently a lawsuit underway against the police department.[88] The city of Minnesota has agreed to pay $20 million to the family of an unarmed woman who was killed by a police officer when she approached his car after he responded to her 911 call.[89]

Neither of the two outcomes listed above solve the problem of police brutality or racial injustice. What many people fail to realize is that in many cities, settlements from lawsuits do not come from police department budgets—they come from taxpayers. Those of us who pay city taxes bear the burden.[90] In fact, police have qualified immunity when it comes to settlements where an accusation of misconduct was made against them while they were on the job. Defunding the police or cutting the amount of money that our government spends on law enforcement and putting that money toward more helpful services, such as fair housing, education, access to health care, and mental health services, is what builds stable, safe, and healthy urban neighborhoods. There is little evidence, if any, to show that providing body cameras and having more police surveillance results in fewer crimes and greater public safety. Funneling the police into communities of color to make arrests only perpetrates more harm and creates trauma. Law enforcement budgets should not outpace community services such as housing and education.[91] For too long now, we have tried to change the misconduct of police officers rather than rethink what the role of police officers should be in cities across the country. Young protestors worldwide have known what to demand from our lawmakers all along: defund the police.

The Sunrise Movement: Addressing Climate Change

We should also take a look at the Sunrise Movement, where a growing number of youth—many of which will be eligible to vote for the first time in their lives—are organizing themselves to get political leaders out of office if they don't act more urgently on climate change. Their method is that of the civil rights movement in the 1960s.[92] They protest quietly in Washington, DC, where police officers zip-tie their hands behind their back and haul them off to jail for disobedience.[93] They have been known to also carry signs that say "your youth is coming for you."[94] Sunrise's mission over the past few years has been to champion the Green New Deal. The Green New Deal is a broad piece of legislation that aims to make the United States a global leader in renewable energy and ensure that future generations are granted their constitutional right to live in a climate system capable of sustaining life.[95]

Young people realize that health disparities and climate change are connected.[96] The reality is that for every form of inequality that exists today, whether it be poverty, hunger, or racism, our health outcomes and our lives are only going to get worse as climate change continues to dry up our resources. I am hopeful that our youth will continue to take to the streets and build up mass mobilization to protest against laws that impact their lives.

Our youth are already confronting daily injustices in the most intimate way just by observing their parents' or guardians' relationships with other adults, such as police officers, underpaid and poorly trained teachers in urban communities, and urban politicians who continuously raise taxes in low-income urban neighborhoods, known as the "poor tax law."[97] The call is for closing the health disparities gap, not widening it; building schools, not prisons, offering health equality, not inadequate health care; providing more teachers and counselors in schools, not police officers; and implementing laws and policies that help, not hinder, urban communities.

Conclusion: We Are Divided into Two Worlds

This book talks about two worlds. The first is the world in which nine families live—the Worleys, the Colemans, the Ruizes, the Rubios, the Blackmons, the Santoyas, the Whittredges, the Stevensons, and the Hugheses—and how policies and legal doctrines have historically harmed these families for decades. The second world is one that is slowly continuing to emerge. It is a world unified in creating health policies and health equity for all people, no matter their race, gender, sexual orientation, ethnicity, or socioeconomic status. But this world requires empathy. Right now, it is the fourth quarter of the championship game, and the former world is winning with no time left on the clock.

The world has become a place where new health policies are passed constantly, but when new leadership takes over, those policies are often repealed or replaced with another policy that is catastrophic, leaving the lives of many hanging in the balance to suffer. The way in which we repeal health policies has caused billions of people living in poverty in urban neighborhoods over the last half-century to have some of the worst health outcomes in society. If we do not do something to counter these policy changes by the next century, the only survivors may be affluent individuals who feel as though they have a sense of entitlement to enforce discriminatory policies that only allow for themselves and their own families to benefit. In just a short period of time, all of the health equality initiatives will be turned on their head, destroying all of the hard work that has been done up to this point to address health inequities and disparities. Maybe we are finally beginning to witness who we really are as a society, but were afraid to admit the truth to ourselves, which is that we are completely divided into two worlds. One world consists of people who have political influence and decision-making power to implement health policies, while the other consists of people experiencing poverty, who will suffer the many consequences of these policies and legal doctrines.

I hope that we choose to work across the nation to advance equitable laws and policies. I hope we come together and invest in big solutions that produce multiple benefits to address the undoing of harmful discriminatory policies that seem to be widening the health equity gap that we have created.

Notes

1. Menakem, *My Grandmother's Hands.*
2. University of Colorado Denver, "Education May Be Key."
3. Mackley, "Top 10 Reasons."
4. "Civil Rights Timeline."
5. "Civil Rights Timeline."
6. "Civil Rights Timeline."
7. "Civil Rights Timeline."
8. The National Council for Black Studies (NCBS) was established in 1975 by African American scholars who understood the need to formalize the African world experience. The NCBS is the only African American organization that provides a platform for scholars, researchers, and community activists to come together, within and outside the discipline, to promote academic excellence and social responsibility.
9. Aiken and Wizner, "Teaching and Doing."
10. Wallace, "Passing the Healthcare Bill."
11. Czukas, "Black Women Experience More Pregnancy Loss."
12. Belnap, "History and Housing."
13. Wood, Goesling, and Avellar, "Effects of Marriage on Health."
14. Cauthen and Fass, "Ten Important Questions."
15. National Geographic Society, "Black Codes and Jim Crow Laws."
16. "Ku Klux Klan."
17. Urofsky, "Jim Crow law."
18. Terrell, "Convict Leasing System."
19. Urofsky, "Jim Crow law."
20. Urofsky, "Jim Crow law."
21. Ann Arbor District Library, "FBI Attacked the Black Panther Party."
22. Dunlap and Johnson, "Setting for the Crack Era."
23. Graff, "Redesigning Racial Caste"; Kennedy and Leonard, "Dealing with Neighborhood Change."
24. Grose, "Rosie Perez."
25. Menakem, *My Grandmother's Hands.*
26. Grose, "Rosie Perez."
27. Grose, "Rosie Perez."
28. "Rosa Parks."
29. Wilson, "Moment When."
30. The Voting Rights Act of 1965 changed the political and socioeconomic status of African Americans in the South, as they were no longer denied the

right to vote based on a literacy test. See "How Selma's Bloody Sunday Became a Turning Point in the Civil Rights Movement."

31. Arenge, Perry, and Clark, "64 Percent of Americans."
32. Herriges, "History of Urban Freeways."
33. Arenge, Perry, and Clark, "64 Percent of Americans."
34. UC Davis Center for Regional Change, "Kern County."
35. Burris, Cloud, and Penn, "Growing Field of Legal Epidemiology."
36. Saha, Arbelaez, and Cooper, "Patient-Physician Relationships."
37. Bertrand and Mullainathan, "Are Emily and Greg More Employable?"
38. Byyny, "Cognitive Bias."
39. The Liaison Committee on Medical Education is the official accrediting body for US and Canadian medical programs. All medical programs must meet the standards of their accreditation services. See Barzansky et al., "Role of Accreditation."
40. Byyny, "Cognitive Bias."
41. Uscher-Pines, Mehrotra, and Chari, "On Call at the Mall."
42. Byyny, "Cognitive Bias."
43. Rose, *Health Disparities, Diversity, and Inclusion.*
44. Rose, *Health Disparities, Diversity, and Inclusion.*
45. Rose, *Health Disparities, Diversity, and Inclusion.*
46. Millsap, "Politicians Deserve Some Blame."
47. Kennedy and Leonard, "Dealing with Neighborhood Change."
48. Millsap, "Politicians Deserve Some Blame."
49. Millsap, "Politicians Deserve Some Blame."
50. Millsap, "Politicians Deserve Some Blame."
51. "Chapter 1: Life Expectancy and Health Life Expectancy."
52. Exworthy, Blane, and Marmot, "Tackling Health Inequalities."
53. Brown, "Stories Artifacts Tell."
54. National Geographic Society, "Natural Selection."
55. Robert Wood Johnson Foundation, "What Is a Culture of Health?"
56. National Institute of Health, "Structural Racism and Discrimination."
57. Exworthy, Blane, and Marmot, "Tackling Health Inequalities."
58. Exworthy, Blane, and Marmot, "Tackling Health Inequalities."
59. Belsky, Melhuish, and Barnes, "Research and Policy."
60. Exworthy, Blane, and Marmot, "Tackling Health Inequalities."
61. Connolly, Baker, and Fellows, "Understanding Health Inequalities."
62. Gillard, "Child Poverty Act 2010."
63. Exworthy, Blane, and Marmot, "Tackling Health Inequalities."
64. Exworthy, Blane, and Marmot, "Tackling Health Inequalities."
65. Batty, "Social Exclusion."
66. Kilduff, "How Poverty."
67. Batty, "Social Exclusion."
68. Wickham et al., "Poverty and Child Health."

69. Berridge, "Policy Response."
70. "FCC fairness doctrine."
71. Berridge, "Policy Response."
72. Yale University, "Selling Smoke."
73. Berridge, "Policy Response."
74. Cullinane, "Marches, Walkouts and Sit-Ins."
75. Berridge, "Policy Response."
76. Smith, Wu, and Murphy, "George Floyd Protests around the World."
77. Berridge, "Policy Response."
78. Berridge, "Policy Response."
79. Garrison, "Young Man."
80. Sharf, "Netflix Creates."
81. Goldman, "Tired of the Killings."
82. Young, "NBA Players."
83. Levin, "These US Cities Defunded Police."
84. Westervelt, "Mental Health and Police Violence."
85. Gray, "Social Worker in the Cop Car."
86. Associated Press, "Proposal Would Use Social Workers."
87. Gray, "Social Worker in the Cop Car."
88. Bonvillian, "Lawsuit."
89. Szekely, "Minneapolis to Pay."
90. Carrega, "Millions in Lawsuit Settlements."
91. Fernandez, "Defunding the Police."
92. Nilsen, "New Face of Climate Activism."
93. Fernandez, "Defunding the Police."
94. Fernandez, "Defunding the Police."
95. Fernandez, "Defunding the Police."
96. Parker, "Support Is Surging."
97. Karger, "'Poverty Tax.'"

Bibliography

Aiken, Jane H., and Stephen Wizner. "Teaching and Doing: The Role of Law School Clinics in Enhancing Access to Justice." *Georgetown Law Faculty Publications and Other Works*, no. 73 (2004): 997–1011. https://scholarship.law.georgetown.edu/facpub/303.

Ann Arbor District Library. "How the FBI Attacked the Black Panther Party." *Ann Arbor Sun*. May 3, 1974. https://aadl.org/node/196860.

Arenge, Andrew, Stephanie Perry, and Dartunorro Clark. "Poll: 64 percent of Americans say racism remains a major problem." *NBC News* (New York, NY), May 29, 2018. https://www.nbcnews.com/politics/politics-news/poll-64-percent-americans-say-racism-remains-major-problem-n877536.

Associated Press. "Proposal Would Use Social Workers, Not LAPD, For Some Calls." *KPBS News* (San Diego, CA), June 17, 2020. https://www.kpbs.org/news/2020/jun/17/proposal-would-use-social-workers-not-lapd-for/.

Barzansky, Barbara, Robert B. Hash, Veronica Catanese, and Donna Waechter. "What Is the Role of Accreditation in Achieving Medical School Diversity?" *AMA Journal of Ethics* 23, no. 12 (2021): E946–52. https://doi.org/10.1001/amajethics.2021.946.

Batty, David. "Social Exclusion: The Issue Explained." *Guardian*. January 15, 2002. https://www.theguardian.com/society/2002/jan/15/socialexclusion1.

Belnap, Meghan. "History and Housing: 4 Benefits of living in a Historic Neighborhood." *RisMedia's Housecall*. November 30, 2018. http://blog.rismedia.com/2018/history-housing-historic-rich-neighborhood/.

Belsky, Jay, Edward Melhuish, and Jacqueline Barnes. "Research and Policy in Developing an Early Years' Initiative: The Case of Sure Start." *International Journal of Child Care and Education Policy*, no. 2 (2008): 1–13. https://doi.org/10.1007/2288-6729-2-2-1.

Berridge, Virginia. "The Policy Response to the Smoking and Lung Cancer Connection in the 1950s and 1960s." *Historical Journal* (Cambridge, England) 49, no. 4 (2006): 1185–209. https://dx.doi.org/10.1017%2FS0018246X06005784.

Bertrand, Marianne, and Sendhil Mullainathan. "Are Emily and Greg More Employable than Lakisha and Jamal? A Field Experiment on Labor Market Discrimination." *The American Economic Review* 94, no. 4 (2004): 991–1013. https://doi.org/10.1257/0002828042002561.

Bonvillian, Crystal. "Lawsuit: Cops 'stomped' on pregnant black woman's stomach, causing miscarriage." *KIRO 7 News* (Seattle, WA). June 1, 2020. https://www.kiro7.com/news/trending/lawsuit-cops-stomped-pregnant-black-womans-stomach-causing-miscarriage/L6GVQZSZHNBQ7LZHPF26ABW52U/.

Brown, Taylor. "The Stories Artifacts Tell: Health and Well-Being at the Field Quarters." Montpelier's Digital Doorway. Last updated July 8, 2020. https://digitaldoorway.montpelier.org/2020/07/08/the-stories-artifacts-tell-health-and-well-being-at-the-field-quarters/.

Burris, Scott, Lindsay K. Cloud, and Matthew Penn. "The Growing Field of Legal Epidemiology." *Journal of Public Health Management and Practice* 26, no. 2 (2020): S4–S9. https://doi.org/10.1097/PHH.0000000000001133.

Byyny, Richard L. "Cognitive Bias: Recognizing and Managing Our Unconscious Biases." *The Pharos* (Winter 2017). https://www.med.upenn.edu/inclusion-and-diversity/assets/user-content/cognitive-bias.pdf.

Carrega, Christina. "Millions in lawsuit settlements are another hidden cost of police misconduct, legal experts say." *ABC News* (Manhattan, NY). July 14, 2020. https://abcnews.go.com/US/millions-lawsuit-settlements-hidden-cost-police-misconduct-legal/story?id=70999540.

Cauthen, Nancy K., and Sarah Fass. "Ten Important Questions about Child-hood Poverty and Family Economic Hardship." National Center for Children in Poverty. Last updated December 2009. https://www.nccp.org/publication/ten-important-questions-about-child-poverty-and-family-economic-hardship/.

"Chapter 1: Life Expectancy and Health Life Expectancy." Public Health England. Last updated July 13, 2017. https://www.gov.uk/government/publications/health-profile-for-england/chapter-1-life-expectancy-and-healthy-life-expectancy.

Chokshi, Dave A. "Income, Poverty, and Health Inequality." *JAMA* 319, no. 13 (2018): 1312–13. https://doi.org/10.1001/jama.2018.2521.

"Civil Rights Timeline." History Channel. Last updated January 19, 2021. https://www.history.com/topics/civil-rights-movement/civil-rights-movement-timeline.

Connolly, Ann Marie, Allan Baker, and Charlotte Fellows. "Understanding Health Inequalities in England." *UK Health Security Agency*. July 13, 2017. https://ukhsa.blog.gov.uk/2017/07/13/understanding-health-inequalities-in-england/.

Cullinane, Susannah. "Marches, Walkouts and Sit-Ins: Gun Control Battle Heads to the Street." *CNN* (Atlanta, GA). February 19, 2018. https://www.cnn.com/2018/02/19/us/florida-parkland-shooting-marches/index.html.

Czukas, Elizabeth. "Why Do Black Women Experience More Pregnancy Loss?" *VeryWell Family*. Last updated April 24, 2021. https://www.verywellfamily.com/why-do-black-women-have-more-pregnancy-losses-2371724.

Delgado, Lyana, Hannah Bills, Ali Segna, Carol Smathers, and Melissa Peters. "Columbus Takes a Stand for Kids' Health." ChangeLab Solutions. February 5, 2019. https://www.changelabsolutions.org/story/columbus-takes-stand-kids-health.

Dunlap, Eloise, and Bruce D. Johnson. "The Setting for the Crack Era: Macro Forces, Micro Consequences (1960–1992)." *Journal of Psychoactive Drugs* 24, no. 4 (1992): 307–21. https://doi.org/10.1080/02791072.1992.10471656.

Exworthy, Mark, David Blane, and Michael Marmot. "Tackling Health Inequalities in the United Kingdom: The Progress and Pitfalls of Policy." *Health Services Research* 38, no. 6, pt. 2 (2003): 1905–22. https://dx.doi.org/10.1111%2Fj.1475-6773.2003.00208.x.

"FCC fairness doctrine." Wikipedia. https://en.wikipedia.org/wiki/FCC_fairness_doctrine.

Fernandez, Paige. "Defunding the Police Will Actually Make Us Safer." *ACLU News* (New York, NY). June 11, 2020. https://www.aclu.org/news/criminal-law-reform/defunding-the-police-will-actually-make-us-safer/.

FindLaw. "Civil Rights: Law and History." FindLaw. Last updated July 24, 2017. https://civilrights.findlaw.com/civil-rights-overview/civil-rights-law-and-history.html.

Freed, Allen E. "Why Do Legal Documents Have to Be So Hard to Understand?" *Paule, Camazine and Blumenthal*. December 16, 2015. https://www.pcblawfirm.com/why-do-legal-documents-have-to-be-so-hard-to-understand/.

Garrison, Greg. "Young Man Who Confronted Police Dogs in 1963 Was Little-Known Civil Rights Icon (Life Stories: Walter Lee Fowlkes)." *Advance Local*. February 22, 2014. https://www.al.com/living/2014/02/young_man_attacked_by_german_s.html.

Gillard, Derek. "Child Poverty Act 2010." Education in England. Last updated November 17, 2020. http://www.educationengland.org.uk/documents/acts/2010-child-poverty-act.html.

Goldman, Tom. "Tired of the Killings: Pro Athletes Refuse to Play to Protest Racial Injustice." *NPR*. August 26, 2020. https://www.npr.org/sections/live-updates-protests-for-racial-justice/2020/08/26/906496470/a-dramatic-day-in-pro-sports-where-the-action-was-no-action.

Graff, Gilda. "Redesigning Racial Caste in America via Mass Incarceration." *The Journal of Psychohistory* 43, no. 2 (2015): 120–33.

Gray, Katti. "The Social Worker in the Cop Car." *CBS News* (New York, NY). April 6, 2015. https://www.cbsnews.com/news/the-social-worker-in-the-cop-car/.

Grose. "Rosie Perez: I'm a Proud Puerto Rican-American and We Need Your Help." *Lenny Letter*. November 29, 2017. https://www.lennyletter.com/story/rosie-perez-proud-puerto-rican-american.

Hassan, Adeel. "Minneapolis to Pay $20 Million to Family of Police Shooting Victim." *New York Times* (New York, NY). May 3, 2019. https://www.nytimes.com/2019/05/03/us/minneapolis-police-shooting.html.

Herriges, Daniel. "The History of Urban Freeways: Who Counts?" *Strong Towns* (Brainerd, MN). February 21, 2017. https://www.strongtowns.org/journal/2017/2/20/the-history-of-urban-freeways-who-counts.

Hewins-Maroney, Barbara, Alice Schumaker, and Ethel Williams. "Health Seeking Behaviors of African Americans: Implications for Health Administration." *Journal of Health and Human Services Administration* 28, no. 1 (2005): 68–95.

"How Selma's Bloody Sunday Became a Turning Point in the Civil Rights Movement." History Channel. Last updated July 18, 2020. https://www.history.com/news/selma-bloody-sunday-attack-civil-rights-movement.

Huston, Aletha C. "Children in Poverty: Can Public Policy Alleviate the Consequences?" *Family Matters*, no. 87 (2011): 13–26.

James, Taj, and Kim McGillicuddy. "Building Youth Movements for Community Change." *Non-profit Quarterly Magazine*. December 21, 2001. https://nonprofitquarterly.org/building-youth-movements-for-community-change/.

Karger, Howard Jacob. "The 'Poverty Tax' and America's Low-Income Households." *Families in Society* 88, no. 3 (2007): 413–17. https://doi.org/10.1606/1044-3894.3650.

Kennedy, Maureen, and Paul Leonard. "Dealing with Neighborhood Change: A Primer on Gentrification and Policy Choices." Brookings Institution Center on Urban and Metropolitan Policy. Accessed May 6, 2020. http://www.policylink .org/sites/default/files/DealingWithGentrification_final.pdf.

Kilduff, Lillian. "How Poverty in the United States is Measured and Why it Matters." Population Reference Bureau. Last updated January 31, 2022. https://www.prb.org/resources/how-poverty-in-the-united-states-is-measured -and-why-it-matters/.

"Ku Klux Klan." History Channel. Last updated February 4, 2022. https://www .history.com/topics/reconstruction/ku-klux-klan.

Law Help. "Legal Aid and Other Low-Cost Legal Help." Legal Aid Society Northeastern New York. Last updated January 6, 2019. https://www.lawhelp .org/resource/legal-aid-and-other-low-cost-legal-help.

Levin, Sam. "These US Cities Defunded Police: 'We're transferring money to the community.'" *Guardian*. March 11, 2021. https://www.theguardian.com /us-news/2021/mar/07/us-cities-defund-police-transferring-money -community.

Mackley, Carter. "Top 10 Reasons Lawyers Produce Hard-To-Read Documents." StartUp Law Talk. Last updated September 17, 2012. https://www .startuplawtalk.com/top-10-reasons-lawyers-produce-hard-to-read-documents/.

Menakem, Resmaa. *My Grandmother's Hands: Racialized Trauma and the Pathway to Mending Our Hearts and Bodies*. Las Vegas, NV: Century Recovery Press, 2017.

Millsap, Adam A. "Politicians Deserve Some Blame for Urban Decline." *Forbes*. August 24, 2016. https://www.forbes.com/sites/adammillsap/2016/08/24 /politicians-deserve-some-blame-for-urban-decline/#3663e2a854c2.

National Geographic Society. "The Black Codes and Jim Crow Laws." *National Geographic*. Last updated April 13, 2020. https://www.nationalgeographic .org/encyclopedia/black-codes-and-jim-crow-laws/.

National Geographic Society. "Natural Selection." *National Geographic*. Last updated October 24, 2019. https://www.nationalgeographic.org/encyclopedia /natural-selection/.

National Institutes of Health. "Structural Racism and Discrimination." National Institute on Minority Health and Health Disparities. Last updated June 14, 2021. https://www.nimhd.nih.gov/resources/understanding-health-disparities /srd.html.

Nilsen, Ella. "The New Face of Climate Activism is Young, Angry, and Effective." *Vox*. Updated September 17, 2019. https://www.vox.com/the-highlight /2019/9/10/20847401/sunrise-movement-climate-change-activist-millennials -global-warming.

Parker, Laura. "Support Is Surging for Teens' Climate Change Lawsuit." *National Geographic* (Washington, DC). March 5, 2019. https://www.nationalgeographic .com/environment/2019/03/youth-climate-change-lawsuit-grows-support/.

Robert Wood Johnson Foundation. "What Is a Culture of Health?" Robert
    Wood Johnson Foundation. Accessed April 20, 2022. https://evidenceforaction
    .org/about-us/what-culture-health.
"Rosa Parks." History Channel. Last updated January 19, 2022. https://www
    .history.com/topics/black-history/rosa-parks.
Rose, Patti Renee. *Health Disparities, Diversity, and Inclusion: Context,
    Controversies, and Solutions.* 1st ed. Burlington, MA: Jones and Bartlett
    Learning, 2018.
Saha, Somnath, Jose J. Arbelaez, and Lisa Cooper. "Patient-Physician Relation-
    ships and Racial Disparities in the Quality of Health Care." *American Journal
    of Public Health* 93, no. 10 (2003): 1713–19. https://doi.org/10.2105/ajph.93
    .10.1713.
Sharf, Zack. "Netflix Creates Black Lives Matter Category with Over 40 Titles:
    'Black Storytelling Matters.'" *IndieWire* (New York, NY). June 10, 2020.
    https://www.indiewire.com/2020/06/netflix-black-lives-matter-page-black
    -storytellers-1202236558/.
Smith, Savannah, Jiachuan Wu, and Joe Murphy. "Map: George Floyd Protests
    around the World." *NBC News.* June 9, 2020. https://www.nbcnews.com
    /news/world/map-george-floyd-protests-countries-worldwide-n1228391.
Stefon, Matt. "Fairness doctrine." In *Encyclopedia Britannica* (online ed.). Last
    modified March 17, 2021. https://www.britannica.com/topic/Fairness-Doctrine.
Szekely, Peter. "Minneapolis to Pay Police Shooting Victim's Family $20
    Million." *Reuters.* May 3, 2019. https://www.reuters.com/article/us-minnesota
    -police/minneapolis-to-pay-police-shooting-victims-family-20-million-idUSKCN
    1S9207.
Terrell, Ellen. "The Convict Leasing System: Slavery in its Worst Aspects."
    Library of Congress. Last updated June 17, 2021. https://blogs.loc.gov/inside
    _adams/2021/06/convict-leasing-system/.
UC Davis Center for Regional Change. "Kern County: Geography of Inequality
    and Opportunities for Action." Last updated October 2017. https://www
    .sierrahealth.org/wp-content/uploads/2021/07/SJVHF_Kern_County_Report
    _Oct_2017.pdf.
University of Colorado Denver. "Education May Be Key to a Healthier, Wealth-
    ier US." *ScienceDaily.* April 29, 2019. https://www.sciencedaily.com/releases
    /2019/04/190429095044.htm.
Urofsky, M. I. "Jim Crow law." In *Encyclopedia Britannica* (online ed.). Last
    modified September 20, 2021. https://www.britannica.com/event/Jim-Crow-law.
Uscher-Pines, Lori, Ateev Mehrotra, and Ramya Chari. "On Call at the Mall: A
    Mixed Methods Study of U.S. Medical Malls." *BMC Health Services Research*
    13, no. 471 (2013): 1–8. https://doi.org/10.1186/1472-6963-13-471.
Wallace, Edward. "Passing the Healthcare Bill from Obama to Trump: More
    Confusion, More Health Disparities." *Journal of Race and Policy* 13, no. 1
    (2017): 61–65.

Wang, Jessica, and Lindsey Huth. "Maps: How Protests Evolved in the Wake of George Floyd's Killing." *Wall Street Journal.* June 12, 2020. https://www.wsj
.com/articles/maps-how-protests-evolved-in-the-wake-of-george-floyds-killing
-11591984846.

Westervelt, Eric. "Mental Health and Police Violence: How Crisis Intervention Teams are Failing." *NPR.* September 18, 2020. https://www.npr.org/2020/09
/18/913229469/mental-health-and-police-violence-how-crisis-intervention
-teams-are-failing.

Wickham, Sophie, Elspeth Anwar, Ben Barr, Catherine Law, and David Taylor-Robinson. "Poverty and Child Health in the UK: using evidence for action." *Archives of Disease in Childhood* 101, no. 8 (2016): 759–66. https://doi.org
/10.1136/archdischild-2014-306746.

Wilson, Christopher. "The Moment When Four Students Sat Down to Take a Stand." *Smithsonian Magazine.* January 31, 2020. https://www
.smithsonianmag.com/smithsonian-institution/lessons-worth-learning-moment
-greensboro-four-sat-down-lunch-counter-180974087/.

Wood, Robert G., Brian Goesling, and Sarah Avellar. "The Effects of Marriage on Health: A Synthesis of Research Evidence." ASPE Research Brief. Last updated June 30, 2007. https://aspe.hhs.gov/reports/effects-marriage-health
-synthesis-recent-research-evidence-research-brief.

Yale University. "Selling Smoke: Tobacco Advertising and Anti-Smoking Campaigns." Yale University Library. Accessed April 20, 2022. https://onlineexhibits
.library.yale.edu/s/sellingsmoke/page/international-anti-smoking-eff.

Young, Dennis. "NBA Players Get Owners to Commit to Turning Arenas into Voting Sites; Playoffs to Resume Saturday." *New York Daily News.* August 28, 2020. https://www.nydailynews.com/sports/basketball/ny-nba-players-owners
-arenas-voting-sites-20200828-ywe4gy6ajbcpfoj6tcei57x3iq-story.html.

ACKNOWLEDGMENTS

As we go about our day-to-day lives with all of our responsibilities, we often miss thanking those who have been pulling for us to succeed in life since day one of our journey. This book could not have been possible without the tremendous support of many people, some of whom are no longer with us. I first want to thank the "Magnificent Seven"—Leonard, Elmida, Dolores, Charles, Arnold, Alvin, and Dorothy—for laying down the foundation of what it means to be the best at your craft. I want to thank my lovely grandmother, Dorothy D. Hargett, who instilled in me the importance of perseverance and hard work. I will never forget what she told me. She said, and I quote, "Just because someone grows up poor, don't mean they don't have value." I also want to thank and dedicate this book to Dr. Terry Kershaw for his wisdom, kindness, and encouragement, which helped me realize that I have a responsibility to share my knowledge with others and an obligation to mentor and uplift the next generations of scholars.

The success of any project, let alone a book, is due to a great amount of empathy, sacrifice, and unconditional love. To the Wallace family, I am grateful to have a family such as you during the writing of this book. You are a constant reminder that a person should never give up and always live out their dream. I want to thank Monique: you have proven to me and the world that a person can do anything in life if they believe in themselves. Thank you for always believing in me and showing me the true meaning of dedication and perseverance. Tatiana and Xavier, I am always moved by both of you and how wonderful you are as young adults. Both of you inspire me to be the best I can be, and I am forever thankful. Tatiana, you continue to be great and use your girl magic every day to show me why it's important to never give up. Your tenacity and work ethic are two of the many things that I admire about you. Xavier, your accomplishments in life continue to make me proud and I enjoy every minute celebrating your greatness. In terms of writing this book, I want to thank my mom and dad. Having both of you travel this journey with me since I was a young child has been nothing but amazing. I appreciate your unconditional love and support. You have given me a strong foundation to stand on, and I hope I continue to make you proud of my accomplishments.

I also want to thank Bob and Priscilla Copeland. Both of you have been key people in my life that have allowed me to do my best. This is something that I do not take lightly. Thank you for all your love and support when it came to writing this book and beyond. To the rest of my family—Davis, Brown, Lewis, Reed, Kershaw, Takeall, Guerino, Merrill, Gant, Hausif, Copeland, Valentine, Burns, Shell, Hinton, Jordan, Murray, Turner, Clark, Wilson, Hickson, Norman, Blake, Tanner, Ferguson, Muniz, Adolf, Perry, Vives, Walker, Ferrell, Moore, Vazquez, and McCollum—I am grateful for your constant support and acts of kindness.

To my colleagues in the Department of Africana Studies at the University of Cincinnati, I want to thank you for your endless support and guidance with this project. I would like to thank Dr. Charles E. Jones for always taking the time to ask, "What is the next project that you will be working on?" These words allowed me to push forward, no matter how many attempts it took to get my project done. I also would like to give thanks to Dr. Earl Wright II for his mentorship and words of confidence. I will never forget when he told me, "No one has ever gotten fired for publishing." I have used these words throughout my career and continue to use them today as my motivation. I wish to recognize and pay a special tribute to Dr. James B. Stewart for his mentorship and encouragement to always promote academic excellence and social responsibility in the discipline of Africana Studies. Thank you, Dr. Stewart—you have been an inspiration before this book, during the writing of the book, and after the book was published. I appreciate you always taking the time to help me excel as a scholar and offering sound advice. I want to give a special thanks to Dr. Monica Adams for collaborating with me on several research projects over the years. Thank you for allowing me to share my thoughts with you as I worked tirelessly on this book project. I appreciate you reading my work and giving me your endless time and feedback during this process.

I also want to give thanks to and acknowledge the following individuals from my Delaware State University family: Ms. Ernestine Brown, Ms. Melody Daniel, Dr. Anthony Hill, Dr. Leela Thomas, Dr. Tom Butler, and Dr. Chavon Dottin. I want to give a special thanks to Dr. Dolores Finger Wright for sharing her ideas and resources with me as I was moving through the process of completing this book.

Finally, I want to thank my editor, Robin W. Coleman, and the entire team at Johns Hopkins University Press for giving me this opportunity to share my research with future generations. I want to say thank you for your endless hard work in marketing the book and getting it out for the public to read.

Free Legal Services for Low-Income Individuals and Families

Law Firm	Description
Alabama	
Legal Services Alabama	Serves people experiencing poverty by providing civil legal aid and promoting collaboration to find solutions to the problems of poverty.
California	
Neighborhood Legal Services of Los Angeles County (NLSLA)	Combats the immediate and long-lasting effects of poverty and expands access to health, opportunity, and justice in Los Angeles' diverse neighborhoods.
Central California Legal Services	A public interest law firm established for the purpose of providing free civil legal assistance to individuals, families, and neighborhoods with lower incomes.
Delaware	
Delaware Community Legal Aid Society	Is committed to racial and ethnic fairness and provides free legal services to victims of housing discrimination, and people living in poverty.
District of Columbia	
Washington Lawyers' Committee for Civil Rights and Urban Affairs	Works to create legal, economic, and social equity through education and public policy.
Legal Aid Society of the District of Columbia	Lawyers that make justice real in individual and systemic ways for persons living in poverty in the District.
Georgia	
Atlanta Legal Aid Society	Helps people with lower incomes meet their basic needs through civil legal assistance by removing barriers.
Illinois	
Legal Assistance Foundation of Metropolitan Chicago	All individuals are entitled to civil legal representation regardless of their income.

(continued)

Law Firm	Description
Maryland	
Maryland Legal Services Corporation	Ensures that Marylanders living in poverty have access to stable, efficient, and effective civil legal assistance.
Maryland Volunteer Lawyers Service	Connects Marylanders with free lawyers to deliver free legal service because there should be justice for all, not just for those who can afford it.
Massachusetts	
Center for Public Representation	Uses legal strategies, advocacy, and policy to promote the integration of full community participation of people who are devalued in society.
Greater Boston Legal Services	Consists of a total of 69 attorneys and 17 paralegals that provide free legal assistance to individuals and families experiencing poverty in the city of Boston.
Michigan	
Michigan Poverty Law Program	Helps alleviate barriers faced by individuals living in poverty by providing civil legal assistance from trained lawyers.
Mississippi	
Mississippi Center for Legal Services	Helps individuals with lower incomes solve legal problems.
New Jersey	
Camden Center for Law and Social Justice	Provides legal assistance to immigrants and those experiencing poverty.
Legal Services of New Jersey	Provides free legal assistance to New Jerseyans living in poverty for their civil legal problems.
New York	
Legal Services NYC	Fights poverty and seeks racial, social, and economic justice for low-income neighborhoods across all five boroughs in New York City.
The Legal Aid Society	Delivers justice in every borough, was built on the belief that no New Yorker should be denied the right to equal justice.
North Carolina	
North Carolina Justice Center	Works on eliminating poverty in North Carolina by ensuring that every household has access to resources, services, and economic security.
Ohio	
Legal Aid Society of Greater Cincinnati	Focuses on resolving serious legal problems for people with lower incomes, and promoting economic and family stability through effective legal assistance.
Ohio Poverty Law Center	Their mission is to reduce poverty and increase justice by protecting the legal rights of Ohioans living, working, and raising their families in poverty.
Pennsylvania	
Pennsylvania Health Law Project	A law firm that represents Pennsylvanians who need help getting or keeping Medicaid.
Community Legal Services of Philadelphia	Their purpose is to fight poverty, challenge systems that perpetuate injustice, and change lives through exceptional legal representation.

Law Firm	Description
Puerto Rico	
Servicios Legales de Puerto Rico	A non-profit organization that provides free legal advice, representation, and education in civil cases to individuals and families experiencing poverty.
Tennessee	
Memphis Area Legal Services	Provide excellence in legal advocacy for those in need.
Tennessee Alliance for Legal Services	Educates policy makers, advocates, and the public about civil legal issues.
Texas	
Lone Star Legal Aid	Protects and advances the civil legal rights of the millions of Texans living in poverty.
Texas Legal Services Center	Works to ensure equal justice for Texans by educating, empowering, and representing vulnerable people, while reshaping the greater legal system that impacts us all.
Virginia	
Virginia Poverty Law Center	Breaks down systemic barriers that keep Virginians trapped in the cycle of poverty through advocacy, education, and litigation.
Virginia Legal Aid Society	A law firm that provides civil legal services to residents experiencing poverty in the area of health care, housing, income, and education.
Washington	
Equal Justice Coalition	Educates policy makers and the public about the importance of civil legal aid while serving people with lower incomes.
Northwest Justice Project	Provides critical civil legal assistance and representation to people living in poverty in cases affecting basic human needs such as access to health care, education, and housing preservation.
West Virginia	
Legal Help for West Virginia	Designed to help members of the public understand the legal system and use it to pursue their just claims.
Legal Aid of West Virginia	Ensures that families living in poverty have an equal shot at justice, in the courtroom and in their communities.
Wisconsin	
Legal Action of Wisconsin	Provides free legal services to people who would otherwise be denied justice.
Wisconsin Equal Justice Fund	Provides pro bono civil legal aid services to families with lower incomes in cases regarding basic needs, such as health and sickness.

University Law School Pro Bono (Volunteer Lawyer) Programs

Brooklyn Law School
Health Law Practice and Policy Clinic
250 Joralemon Street, Brooklyn, NY 11201
https://brooklaw.edu/

Case Western Reserve University School of Law
Health Law Clinic
11075 East Boulevard, Cleveland, OH 44106
https://case.edu/law/

Columbia Law School
Health Justice Advocacy Clinic
435 W 116th Street, New York, NY 10027
https://law.columbia.edu/

Florida International University College of Law
Health Law and Policy Clinic
11200 SW 8th Street, Green Library Room 475, Miami, FL 33199
https://law.fiu.edu/

Georgetown University Law Center
Health Justice Alliance Clinic
600 New Jersey Avenue NW, Washington, DC 20001
https://law.georgetown.edu/experiential-learning/clinics/our-clinics
/health-justice-alliance-clinic/

Mitchell Hamline School of Law
Health Law Clinic
875 Summit Avenue, St. Paul, MN 55105
https://mitchellhamline.edu/

New York Law School
Poverty Law Clinic
185 W Broadway, New York, NY 10013
https://nyls.edu/

Quinnipiac University School of Law (Mount Carmel Campus)
Health Law Clinic
275 Mount Carmel Avenue, Hamden, CT 06518
https://qu.edu/schools/law/

Rutgers Law School (Newark Campus)
Urban Legal Clinic
123 Washington Street, Newark, NJ 07102
https://law.rutgers.edu/

Saint Louis University School of Law
Health Law Clinic
100 N Tucker Blvd., Suite 942, St. Louis, MO 63101
https://slu.edu/law/health/index.php

University of Connecticut School of Law
Health Law and Public Law
55 Elizabeth Street, Hartford, CT 06105
https://uconn.edu/#

University of Kansas School of Law
Family Healthcare Legal Services Clinic
Public Policy Clinic
1535 W 15th Street, Lawrence, KS 66045
https://law.ku.edu/

University of Pittsburgh School of Law
Health Law Clinic
3900 Forbes Avenue, Pittsburgh, PA 15260
https://www.law.pitt.edu/about/engaged/health-law-clinic

marriage and mental health, 135
masturbation, 55
maternal mortality, 134–35
media stigmatization of people in poverty, 77–79
Medicaid: and abortion, 62; and dentistry, ix, 36–38, 41; expansion of, xi; and hospital closures, 80; and "no duty to treat" policy, 41; problems overview, 108–9; spending by, 108
medical licenses, 40
Medicare, 41, 80, 109–12
Medicare Advantage, 111–12
Medicare for All Act, xi
mental health: access to care, x; and cockroach infestations, 21; and historical timeline of African Americans, 135–37; and incarceration, 87–88; and marriage, 135; and maternal mortality, 134–35; police response to, 156; and police violence, 90–91, 92; and poor school infrastructure, 150; and poverty, 65. See also trauma
methodology, 3–4
miscarriage, 134
MORE Health Education Act, 119
mortality: and carbon monoxide, 26; and COVID-19, vii, 24–25; and disparities in insurance coverage, vii, 66–67; and environmental hazards, 19; and heat, ix; infant, 17; maternal, 134–35; and oral health, 36; and police violence, 156–57; and poverty, 65, 66–67
mouthwash, 34, 35

National Basketball Association (NBA), 153–54
National School Breakfast Program, 118
National School Lunch Program, 118
natural selection, 147
Navy and environmental contamination on Puerto Rico, 18–20, 49
NBA (National Basketball Association), 153–54
Netflix, 153
New York City Housing Authority, 20, 21
Nixon, Richard, 30n9

"no duty to treat" policy, 39–42
nuisance, law of, 28–29

Obama, Barack, 79, 133
obesity: and access to quality food, 11, 48, 49; in children, 57, 116; and COVID-19 pandemic, viii; and culture, 6, 50–51; in family stories, 6–7, 10–11, 48–51, 54, 56; and geography, 48–53; programs, 116–18; rates and poverty, 57
opioid policy, 94
oral health disparities, ix, 33–42
Ortiz, Ramon, 7, 47
overcrowding, 16–18

Parks, Rosa, 138
Pérez-Stable, Eliseo J., 115
physicians. See health care providers and physicians
police: body cameras, 157; "defund the police," 155–58; police violence, 90–91, 92, 151–53, 154–58; and qualified immunity, 154–55, 157; and stop-and-frisk, 75
policies: and antismoking movement, 149–50; challenges in making, 120–21, 128–30; and cockroach infestations, 21; and community initiatives, 140; education, 62–63, 86, 118, 143, 150–51; and enforcement, 130; engagement with, 130–32, 140; environmental, 120, 158; as focus of author, 2–3; importance of, xi–xii, 120–21, 128–32, 159–60; "no duty to treat" policy, 39–42; opioid policy, 94; questions for, 4; as school subject, 5; trauma, 93–96; and youth movement, 151–58. See also programs
pollution: air pollution, 16–20; and gas stoves, 25–26; and heat islands, ix; and overcrowding, 16–18; and secondhand smoke, 26–29
post-traumatic stress disorder (PTSD), 92
poverty: and children, xi, 68; and children in UK, 148–49; and COVID-19, ix; cycle of, 63–65, 84–86; determining levels of, x, 105, 148–49; and hypertension rates, 57; increase

poverty (*continued*)
    in, 57; and increase in inequality, 65;
    lack of protections in Constitution,
    58–63; and life expectancy, 68; media
    portrayals of, 77–79; and mortality,
    65, 66–67; and obesity rates, 57; race
    and rates of, ix; and spatial racism,
    84–86; and stigmatization, 77–79
pregnancy: maternal mortality, 134–35;
    teenage, 55
primary care physicians, x. *See also*
    health care providers and physicians
programs: Aid to Families with
    Dependent Children, x, 104; Child
    Tax Credit, xi; Earned Income Tax
    Credit, x, xi, 114–15; housing,
    112–14; obesity, 116–18; overview of,
    x; Social Security Disability Insurance,
    106–8; Supplemental Nutritional
    Assistance Program, 115–16, 117;
    Temporary Assistance for Needy
    Families, x, 104–6; in UK, 148–49;
    and work requirements, 104–5, 108.
    See also Medicaid; Medicare
protests: Black Lives Matter, 151–53;
    civil rights movement, 131, 136,
    138–39, 152–53; climate change, 158;
    "defund the police," 155–58; whites
    and 152–53
PTSD (post-traumatic stress disorder),
    92
Public Health Cigarette Smoking Act,
    30n28
Puerto Rico, contamination in, 18–20, 49

qualified immunity, 154–55, 157

race: and COVID-19, vii–viii, 24–25; in
    demographic projections, 145; and food
    insecurity rates, 58; and gentrification,
    145–46; and hospitalizations, vii; and
    hypertension, 51, 52, 53, 54, 55; and
    insurance, vii, 133; and maternal
    mortality, 134–35; and media
    portrayals of people in poverty, 78–79;
    and oral health disparities, 35–42; and
    poverty rates, ix; as research focus, 2;
    and veteran health care, 60; and violent
    crime victimization, 88, 89

racism and discrimination: and Great
    Migration, 15–16; and Hispanics,
    137–38; in historical timeline of
    African Americans, 136–37; and
    implicit bias, 141–43; Jim Crow laws,
    131, 136; and media portrayals of
    people in poverty, 78–79; and oral
    health, 36, 42; and police violence,
    90–91, 92, 151–53, 154–58; public
    opinion on, 139; Sheila Blackmon on,
    9; spatial racism, 84–86; and
    stop-and-frisk, 75; Tulsa, OK
    massacre, 83–84. *See also* civil rights
    movement
Reconstruction, 131, 136
*Report of the Secretary's Task Force on
    Black and Minority Health,* 1
resilience, 128, 137, 138
Rich, Adrienne, 58
rights: to education, 63; to health care,
    39; lack of protections for the poor,
    58–63; and legal counsel, 113–14;
    voting, 138
Robert Wood Johnson Foundation, 42
rodents, 17
Rubio family, 12–13; and environmental
    hazards, 20–21; and food insecurity,
    46; and insurance, 66; and oral health,
    38; and police violence, 90; on
    poverty, 68
Ruckelshaus, William, 29n9
Ruiz family, 8; and cultural competency,
    144–45; and environmental hazards,
    18–20; and hypertension, 50, 63; and
    obesity, 49–51; and oral health, 35,
    38–39, 42; and toll of poverty, 63–64;
    and trauma, 91

salt. *See* sodium
San Antonio v. Rodriguez, 62–63
Santoya, Rosa, 6–7; and diabetes, 54; on
    discrimination, 137–38; and obesity,
    6–7, 54; on treatment of non-white
    veterans, 60
schools. *See* education and schools
secondhand smoke, 26–29
segregation: in Greenwood, OK, 83–84;
    Jim Crow laws, 131, 136; policy, 131.
    See also civil rights movement

Whitehouse, Sheldon, 99n82

Whittredge family, 10–11; and diet, 11, 51; and education, 129–30; and empty buildings, 144; and insurance, 67, 111; and obesity, 10–11, 49; and oral health, 37–38

women: and maternal mortality, 134–35; and sexual violence, 93, 95

work. *See* employment

Worley family, 11–12; and diabetes, 48; and environmental hazards, 17–18; and hospital closures, 81–82; and obesity, 48; and oral health, 35; and trauma, 87, 96–97

youth movement, 151–58